HEALING ENERGY

MASTER ZI SHENG WANG
&
TIBETAN BUDDHIST QIGONG

BY
VIRGINIA NEWTON

HEALING ENERGY:
MASTER ZI SHENG WANG
&
TIBETAN BUDDHIST QIGONG

BY
VIRGINIA NEWTON

CHINA BOOKS & PERIODICALS, INC.

Grand Master Khenpo Munsel Rinpoche, eighth generation lineage holder of Guru Padmasambhava's teachings. Padmasambhava, the father of Tibetan Buddhism, brought Qigong teachings to Tibet.

Master Zi Sheng Wang was directed by his beloved teacher, Grand Master Khenpo Munsel Rinpoche, to bring Tibetan Qigong teachings to the west.

Library of Congress Cataloging-in-Publication Data

Newton, Virginia.
    Healing energy: the Tibetan Buddhist qigong of Master Zi Sheng Wang / by Virginia Newton.
    p. cm.
ISBN 0-8351-2679-X (pbk.: alk. paper)
    1. Qi gong--Therapeutic use. 2. Wang, Zi Sheng, 1930- 3. Exercise therapy. I. Title.

RM727.C54 N48 2001
615.8'2--dc21

00-065937

Printed in Canada

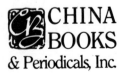

CHINA BOOKS & Periodicals, Inc.

2929 Twenty-Fourth Street
San Francisco, CA 94110
415-282-2994
www.chinabooks.com

I dedicate this book to my husband and life partner Tom...my creative work is enriched through his unfailing love and support. I also dedicate this book to Master Wang in hope that it will further his mission in the west, and to all beings in hope that they might find peace and healing through Tibetan Qigong.

Acknowledgements

I would like to express my deep appreciation to Master Zi Sheng Wang for placing his faith in me to write this book, and for all of the many important lessons he is helping me to learn. Thanks also to his wife, Houxia Song, for generously sharing her article "Miraculous Tibetan Kung Fu and Professor Zi Sheng Wang," and allowing me to use this material as a basis for Chapter One. Her quiet and loving support of Master Wang's work provides a role model for his many students.

My sincere thanks to Charles Law for his generosity in bringing this book to publication, and for his ongoing legal counsel to Master Wang and to the International Tibetan Qigong Association (ITQA). I am grateful to Carol Ann Wang (no relation to Master Wang) for her persistence in trying to verify with Tibetan Buddhist scholars the historical accuracy and English spellings of the Nyingma lineage. I am indebted to Master Wang's many Chinese and Tibetan disciples because without them and their early financial support, the American chapter of Master Wang's incredible story could not have been written. I am also indebted to my American Dharma brothers and sisters (too many to list here but you know who you are) who have worked so hard this past five years to lay a strong foundation for ITQA.

Great respect and gratitude are reserved for those brave individuals who have opened their lives and shared their stories so this book could be written. I have spoken to and read evaluations and testimonials from hundreds of people who have been helped through Master Wang's healing sessions. Many of those people were willing to help with this book; however, in defining the scope of this project I could select only a few for in-depth interviews. To all of those who were willing to come forward, my thanks and my hope that you are continuing to heal.

Virginia Newton
Soquel, CA

Being a Buddhist for over 20 years, I have the honor for the first time to sponsor publication of a book regarding this remarkable religion. Master Wang is a part of the Buddhism. Through his incredible Tibetan Buddhist Qigong and energy, he leads people to enter the gate of the universe.

This book is a bridge to connect Master Wang and the people of the west. When we fully learn the spirit of this healing energy and Buddhism, we will be able to heal our own body and soul. The builder of this bridge, Virginia Newton, shall receive all blessing for creating this wonderful work. I wish more bridges can be built by her and others in the future. I can be counted on to provide the most support that I am able to give.

Charles Law

Contents

Introduction

Qigong is a school of practical science that cultivates the body and the mind. It has embedded itself completely into the culture of China and guided and influenced Chinese medical science, religion, martial arts, astronomy, philosophy and literature for thousands of years. In Master Zi Sheng Wang's book, *The Path of Dzogchen*, he relates that the earliest writings about Qigong indicate that it was first used as a dance or a kind of movement to guide the flow of blood in the arteries and veins, clear and aid the joints, and prevent disease. Around 5,000 BC the wise man Fuxi of the ancient Chinese Xia clan summarized the results that people had reached from their observation and research of the relationship between the human body and all things in the universe. This took form as the "bagua" (the eight diagrams) which revealed the profound laws of constant change in the universe and the principle of observation and deduction, and became the most basic theory of ancient Chinese civilization.

There are numerous forms of Qigong and thousands of Qigong teachers in China, as well as in the west. Some are real, some are fakes who make claims to miracles they cannot produce. Although most forms of Qigong can produce energy, the level of this energy varies widely among Qigong masters, as does their healing results. Many lower level Qigong masters have acquired their skills from less accomplished teachers or Qigong masters without lineage. Lineage is essential for the highest levels of attainment. The higher forms, such as Taoist Qigong and Tibetan Buddhist Qigong, can trace their purity through an unbroken lineage back through the centuries. Tibetan Buddhist Qigong is considered the highest form because it was kept very pure for generations due to the inaccessibility of the region, and because it was maintained as a secret teaching taught only to the highest level Nyingma practitioners.

During my professional career as Continuing Education Specialist and Director of Arts and Humanities at the University of California Santa Cruz Extension, I learned to carefully evaluate potential instructors before engaging them to teach. Although a person might seem from their resume to possess the necessary qualifications, I found it was important to personally assess their teaching skills before making a final selection. The best instructors invariably possess a quality that I have come to recognize as "qi" (pronounced "chee"), an abundant level of energy that sets them apart from their peers.

After I retired from the university in 1995, I was free to devote myself fully to my own creative work and to explore other lifelong areas of interest. It was during this initial year of exploration that I encountered a retired university professor from Beijing, Master Zi Sheng Wang, and his special form of energy teaching. As I experienced it for myself, I noticed improvement in my own energy, and I saw dramatic improvement in the health and energy of other participants with severe illness. I realized that the energy Master Wang creates and emits to others is highly unusual.

For example, during one session he left the building completely, climbed a hill behind the facility and sent energy to us from this remote location. Many people were doubtful about whether this was going to work, so to dispel any doubt Master Wang sent extra energy from the hilltop. The energy we experienced during this session was so palpable and strong it felt like a hurricane was occurring inside the room, and I feared the roof was going to fly off the building!

America is recognized worldwide as the leader in science and technology. If our advanced technology could somehow be interwoven with the powerful energy of Tibetan Buddhist Qigong, I believe there could be astounding results, especially in the areas of health and healing. It is my hope that this book can bring attention to Master Wang and this powerful form of healing energy.

Although my early education and training as a journalist taught me to be rigorous in seeking and reporting facts, as an artist and creator I have always been interested in intuitive knowledge, the kind of wisdom that comes to us seemingly from nowhere, that I have come to respect as the wellspring of creativity. I was probably influenced in this regard as a child by the rich spiritual life of my southern ancestors, especially my Methodist minister grandfather and my grandmother who was a descendant of early French settlers and the Indians of western Louisiana. Perhaps it is this blend of spirituality, intuition and truth seeking that led me to this ancient practice and ultimately to write this book.

In my work on the book I decided to let the people who benefited directly from this experience speak for themselves, in their own words, through in-depth interviews. I have included a brief summary of my own very basic understandings about the Nyingma Tibetan Buddhist tradition. These understandings come from my notes of Master Wang's teachings as well as my research of various other Nyingma writings. Dharma is a vast subject with many thousands of complex texts, most of which have not been translated for western readers. I do not represent myself as a Buddhist scholar, therefore any errors, omissions, or misunderstandings are my own and should not be attributed to Master Wang.

• • •

In Buddhism, three is an important number. In March, 1996, a friend told me about an upcoming Qigong workshop taught by Master Zi Sheng Wang at Land of Medicine Buddha, a Tibetan Buddhist retreat center near my home in Soquel, California. A few days later I read an announcement about the class in the weekly paper, but still didn't sign up. The day before the workshop, I saw another small listing in the events calendar of the paper, and immediately made plans to attend.

I have long since stopped questioning exactly why I responded to this third "invitation." Why I somehow felt that I must attend the workshop. I certainly was not looking for a guru or teacher. I knew very little about Buddhism, Qigong or alternative forms of healing. All I had to go on was my experience of traveling in China a few months before.

Early mornings in Beijing I found myself in the Purple Bamboo Park across the street from my hotel, walking and observing throngs of people of all ages doing Tai Chi and Qigong. These gentle forms of moving meditation fascinated me, and several times I was invited to participate. I was clumsy and unable to keep up with the flowing movements, but even this awkward beginning gave me a sense of the balance and well-being that comes with the movement of qi or energy.

A week later on Mount Huang Shan in Anhui province, I hugged "Flying Over Rock" for luck, pressed my forehead into its damp granite surface for wisdom, and thought about the monks and artists that had meditated and created in this place for centuries. It was a damp afternoon with swirling mist and gusts of rain. I stood atop an odd shaped rock at a small pavilion nearby and held my arms out. The moisture laden clouds enveloped me. I was startled to feel a jolt of energy flowing through me. I felt as if my body had ceased to exist, that my spirit merged with the wild clouds and the immortal stone beneath my feet. Later, warm and dry in my tiny room in the Behei Guesthouse I felt like a pilgrim who had come for and received a miracle. But at the time I had little context for understanding this experience.

Master Wang accepted his first group of American disciples in early 1996 a short time after his first American workshops in North Dakota, Massachusetts, Oregon and California. The March class I attended was his second California workshop, and included a review of the first teaching. I attended his next workshops in April and May, and I diligently practiced all I had learned.

During the May workshop I decided to become a disciple. It was both a spontaneous and a well considered decision. My whole life felt like preparation. I suddenly knew that the events of this life, and probably of past lives, had prepared me to embark on this spiritual journey. Although I knew there was to be a disciple initiation ceremony that weekend, I had not expected to be included in it. Most of the others in this "second patch" of disciples had been preparing for several months. I am normally a very skeptical and cautious person, so I am still surprised at myself for letting go and trusting enough to join them.

We knew very little at that point about Master Wang or what it truly meant to become a disciple. Most thought it mainly meant being allowed to learn more advanced forms of the ancient Tibetan Buddhist Qigong that he had come here to teach. But my intuition told me that this decision was life-altering and carried with it an awesome responsibility. I had to look deep within myself and ask if I could not only live up to the five Buddhist precepts, but if I could also accept this great responsibility. Any remaining doubt was erased by an inner voice that told me to simply open my heart and do whatever felt right. Once the decision was made I had a profound sense of well-being and a strong feeling that I would be fine if I kept my intentions pure and let my heart always be my guide. Nothing more, nothing less, would be expected.

That first year Master Wang meditated a great deal about whether or not it would be proper for him to teach American students Six Syllable Mantra, a second level practice, so soon. In the traditional way of receiving these sacred teachings, it takes a student many years of practice before progressing to the more advanced levels. Ultimately, he received a "transmission" of approval from his departed teacher, the venerable Grand Master Khenpo Munsel Rinpoche, and the workshop was scheduled.

We were all nervous and excited as he began the purification ceremony, a meditation that lasted for most of an entire day. The meditation included listening to an audio tape of Master Wang's Tibetan Dharma brothers chanting the 100 Syllable Mantra. Soon after this ceremony began, I entered a deep Qigong meditative state. At one point Master Wang approached me and placed an ancient mala (prayer beads) around my neck.

About three hours into the ceremony the chanting changed. We had been told that the last part of the tape contained the only recorded incantation of this sacred mantra by the Grand Master. As soon as I heard his voice resonate I experienced a physical impact on my forehead. It felt as if a shadowy figure had hurled a fragrant flower, a white lotus, directly at me.

Often during meditation or practice a sense of awareness or realization moves the practitioner up into a higher level of consciousness. The instant my awareness connected the impact on my forehead with the white lotus, I was immediately "transported" to Tibet into the midst of some other ritual. Kneeling in a group of chanting monks, I saw the hems of purple and gold robes. I was suddenly thrust to the center of the group and handed a bundle wrapped in tea-colored silk. As I unwrapped it, I was stunned to realize the bundle contained human bones. Overwhelmed at being singled out for this gift I had a profound sense of remembrance and began to cry. The head lama paused in his incantation, took my hand and placed the skull on my palm. He carefully rewrapped the remaining bones in the silk and pressed the bundle to my heart.

When I was asked by Master Wang to write this book I felt very honored, but overwhelmed at being singled out for this task. My rational mind began to think of the many reasons I was not the person he should have chosen: I still consider myself a novice to Buddhism and Qigong. I do not have a scientific or medical background, nor am I a healer. I already have far too many projects on my plate. Although I am a writer, I have never before authored a book.

During meditation a few days later, I suddenly began to laugh. My awareness focused on three teachers who are important to me, Master Wang, the Grand Master, and another lama I recognize in meditation only as "Third Master." They were all looking down at me in a very perplexed way wondering why I continued to doubt their wisdom in choosing me for this task. My perception shifted and an inner voice came to me clearly: *Just go ahead. Begin. It will all come together in the work.*

So, once again I let go of my fears, placed my trust in the universe and began this book. I am only the vehicle. The stories in this book are not mine. They belong to Master Wang and to those people who have experienced incredible healing through him. I trust that if I keep my heart open these stories will transcend my own limitations and direct the reader toward the ancient practice of Tibetan Buddhist Qigong, an important path of healing.

1 The Rainbow Bridge

The Tibetan plateau, known as the "roof of the world," is surrounded by an extensive mountain range and shrouded by a veil of mystery. Over the centuries all but the most adventurous travelers have been kept away from Tibet due to the harsh and unpredictable weather, the thin air of high altitudes, and the wild animals that roam this sparsely populated land.

Among Tibet's many secrets, Tantric Buddhism and Tantric Kung Fu are among its most precious. Kung Fu refers to the special or miraculous abilities of high level practitioners. Among these special abilities "rainbow body" is considered one of Tantric Buddhism's highest achievements. Rainbow body refers to a phenomenon that occurs at the time of death as the five gross elements that form the physical body dissolve back into their essences of five colored lights. In the Nyingma tradition rainbow body symbolizes the attainment of Buddhahood, possible in one lifetime. This can only be achieved by a devoted practitioner of the Dzogchen practice of Thogal who has mastered the highest level and exhausted all grasping and fixation. For those who have mastered a slightly lower level of this advanced practice, sometimes the hair and nails will remain.

Over the past thousand years, only the most dedicated practitioners have achieved rainbow body. In September 1998, another Tibetan Tantric practitioner, Khenpo Ahehue, achieved rainbow body. There were no remains left at his death, only rainbow colored light.

Scientists have long been inspired to do extensive research into this phenomenon, and many others have had a strong desire to receive the Tantric Dharma teachings. Very few have reached their goal, however, due to the inaccessibility of the most advanced practitioners in the high mountains of Tibet. Since the nineteenth century only a few non-Tibetans, such as the Chinese Masters Nan Hai and Guan Kung, have had the strong karmic connection and perseverance to overcome the many hardships that must be endured in order to receive these teachings. Master Zi Sheng Wang is one of the very few non-Tibetan practitioners who has received these teachings in modern times.

Zi Sheng Wang was born in Beijing in 1930. At age nine he became seriously ill, a result of the severe famine that swept China in the wake of war and invasion. Thinking that their son was dying, his parents left him at a Buddhist monastery for final purification rites. Instead, the monks were able to cure the boy of his physical problems using Qigong and Buddhist practices. This experience set him on a life-long path of Buddhism. As a teenager he was sent to study at an American Christian missionary school, which gave him knowledge of the world beyond China. He continued his study of Qigong with various masters, and as a young man he became a top athlete. Athletics became his profession and ultimately he became an assistant professor and coach teaching elite athletes at a branch of the People's University of Beijing.

By 1950, his healing skills through the use of Qigong were already quite notable. By now a university professor, it was politically dangerous for Master Wang to affiliate with Buddhist practices. However, despite the danger he discreetly continued his Buddhist study and practice. During a meditation he had a vision in which he was given instructions to find a particular lama of the Tibetan Nyingma Buddhist tradition. After several years of searching he found Grand Master Khenpo Munsel Rinpoche, the lama he was seeking, in a very remote region of Tibet.

Master Wang conquered many obstacles and difficulties to finally become a true disciple of this highly respected Rinpoche, the eighth generation lineage holder of Guru Padmasambhava's lineage. Thereafter for more than 40 years, Master Wang made several difficult journeys each year to Tibet to study with his beloved teacher. During his half-century of devotion and intensive study, he received a complete transmission of a unique and ancient healing system, Tibetan Buddhist Qigong. Through his high level of practice he also accomplished the great "siddhi" (miraculous power), the union of emptiness and clarity.

Tibetan Buddhist Qigong allows one to access the healing powers of nature. Through this practice one can achieve one's greatest potential, unravel natural wisdom and develop profound spiritual awareness. Tibetan Buddhist Qigong acknowledges the connectedness of body, mind and spirit to health and illness and focuses these elements into powerful healing energy. Dedicated practice helps to build up the qi, or energy field, dissolves tension and stress, and allows realization of optimum health.

Due to the many dangers inherent for a Chinese citizen involved in Tibetan Buddhist practice, for many years Master Wang never exposed his high accomplishment. He just practiced faithfully and kept it to himself. But following his Guru's wishes, during the 1980s Master Wang began to apply these Tantric methods to benefit human beings. He used Tibetan Buddhist Qigong to promote health and longevity and balance yin and yang energy in the body to overcome disease. His healing talent and spiritual attainment began to be noticed by the public, and he began to accept his own disciples.

Master Wang was able to combine teachings he had received from Taoist Qigong masters with the high level Vajrayana teachings received from his Tibetan master. He discovered that he could use acupuncture needles on a small human effigy to transmit healing energy and effect change without touching a person's body. He studied acupuncture meridians and developed what he calls "needleless healing," a unique non-invasive method he uses in healing thousands of people at one time, even across vast distances.

Until recently, the advanced practices of Tibetan Buddhist Qigong have been available only to a select group of Nyingma lamas in Tibet. Before he departed this life in 1994, Grand Master Khenpo Munsel bestowed on Master Wang the formal title of Rinpoche (highest level teacher) along with many of his Dharma objects and treasures. The Grand Master also directed him to go and spread these very sacred teachings in the west so they would not be lost to the world.

In 1995, Master Wang was invited to the United States to conduct healing sessions in Fargo, North Dakota; Boston, Massachusetts; Portland, Oregon and many California cities. He also traveled to Canada where he sent healing energy to more than ten thousand people. Master Wang's energy sessions produce astounding results. He has helped thousands of people regain their health, including people with terminal cancer, AIDS, stroke, paralysis, Parkinson's, and many other types of illness.

Master Wang has authored a book, *The Path of Dzogchen*, published in China. An English translation is planned. He was honored as the Most Outstanding Qigong Master of the Year in 1998 by the International Congress of Chinese Medicine. He has also created a non-profit organization, the International Tibetan Qigong Association (ITQA) with headquarters in San Francisco, California, for the purpose of teaching Tibetan Buddhist Qigong to his many American disciples and students. Master Wang continues to travel to the high regions of Tibet several times each year to assist lamas, conduct healings and pay tribute at the shrine of his departed master. He is working with his Tibetan Dharma brothers to build a bridge and dormitories at the site to make it more accessible for western students who wish to study higher levels of Tibetan Buddhist Qigong.

These ancient and sacred Nyingma Tantric practices that Master Wang has mastered and now shares with us link our culture with Tibetan Buddhist culture. This link is a crucial bridge, a "rainbow" bridge, to promote understanding and cooperation between the healing practices of east and west for the benefit of all humanity.

2 Miraculous Recovery

I interviewed John at his home on several acres where the flat farmlands of California's Salinas Valley lap up to the Gavilans. The summer day was warm but cooled by a breeze that blew in from the coast. We sat around a table outside on a covered patio area overlooking his neighbor's young vineyard. Cattle grazed on the green hills beyond.

John is not old, but his face shows the effects of his outdoor life. The creases that have been etched around his eyes and mouth through pain are gradually softening. His lifelong demeanor as a "tough guy" is also softening as he explores the path of Tibetan Buddhist Qigong.

The original damage was a broken leg that occurred in 1950 in a motorcycle accident. It particularly damaged the left leg and they were going to amputate it below the knee, but ultimately did not. The leg had a number of breaks, and when they put it back together, it took several operations over a period of about two years. Ultimately the leg ended up an inch shorter as well as having damage to the knee and the ankle. Over the years I've damaged it since, motorcycling and parachuting and what have you. And probably 20 years ago or more, the use of the knee became very minimal. I could not bend the knee more than about three or four inches because of pain. It limited the things I could do. I couldn't run, climbing stairs was difficult. I mean life was OK, but it certainly put some parameters on my activities. I was mostly in constant pain, from mild to severe if it got twisted wrong.

The doctor who saved my leg had just come back from the second world war and had seen the Germans using metal in the femur. They did that, and that's what saved the leg ultimately. But in the years after that I damaged it several more times and they finally removed the cartilage totally. Over the years where the bones were rubbing together, it was rubbing into the nerves and that's where the pain came from. But the outlook of it from the standpoint of the western medical profession was to take pain pills and eventually we'll give you an artificial knee.

I first encountered Master Wang at a healing session in Mountain View, California, about a year and a half ago. Sort of off the Qigong subject but I still race motorcycles, and I was injured in Colorado. After they let me out of the hospital and I was on my way home, I called my wife on the cell phone from just outside of Las Vegas and I told her I was in a lot of pain. My wife is a Reiki practitioner and so she sent me Reiki healing energy and it took the pain away. When I returned home, she taught me how to do Reiki and I've used it quite effectively. And when she became involved in Qigong, she was telling me about Master Wang's healing sessions and so I went. Probably by her persuading me to go the first time, I guess you'd have to say that. But I didn't go there with any intent of fixing my knee. I was resolved with the outcome that someday I'd have to get a metal knee.

The thing is that I've broken everything at some time or another, so a lot of things don't work very well. So any help on anything would have been good. I had not even thought about the knee. I knew it hurt and it didn't work very well, but I had not gone there for that purpose.

I realized the first time I met him that Master Wang was a special person, so I continued to attend healing sessions and a few workshops. I noticed changes, subtle changes, not necessarily in the knee but just with my outlook on life and my whole life in general. I saw colors during the healings, but not as readily as most people. And I wasn't jumping around with spontaneous movement or any of that. But I would see colors sometimes and different things.

Also during that time, I had a malfunction parachuting and broke a rib and messed up my back, moved a bunch of vertebrae around. The medical people had worked on it and said that was the best it was going to get, and the orthopedic surgeon said they could go in and pin it. But I said, no, I don't want to do that. I had a nerve getting pinched or whatever. The chiropractor I usually go to did quite a good job, but it still was messed up. And at one of the healings, I don't remember which one, I was sitting there about half way through. Like I say, I don't normally get much spontaneous movement, but I started wiggling around and my body started moving and I could feel this pop, pop, pop, pop, and it's been fine every since.

A few months ago I was at a workshop in San Francisco. We did the group healing in the morning, and in the afternoon there was a teaching, One Finger Zen Part One. Master Wang demonstrated the practice and explained what it was about. Then we had a practice session and they divided us into groups. They had nine different stations in the open area of the large room. A disciple was located at each station and they would go through that one position over and over with people as they would come around. It was a very good process. I was going around to each one, probably 40 minutes of going around and practicing. And those positions that required deep knee bends were really rough.

It was kind of bend a little bit of that knee, and kind of squat on the other side, a very ugly looking positioning for me. Other people there who had seen me before realized that I limped and they just took it for granted that I couldn't really do those positions. And then about 40 minutes into this practice session, I felt a hand on my shoulder. It was Master Wang. He said, "Follow me." I thought, maybe I'm being thrown out because I wasn't doing it very well. And we walked up to the front of the room, between the chairs and the stage. I was following him and he turned around so we were face to face, maybe three or four feet apart. He said, "You follow, no problem." He looked me right in the eye when he said that, and I said, "OK."

At that moment, my mind was blank. I didn't know what we were going to do. Follow? Yes I'll follow, but very quickly we started doing Three Palms and started doing the One Finger Zen movements. I thought, oh no, what are we going to do when we come to the deep knee bends? That first squatting posture, we were right eye to eye when we came to that. He started down and I started down. I went right down, squatted right down. All the way down and back up. I just couldn't believe it!

In the meantime, many of the people who were practicing were watching because when Master Wang walks around or takes hold of somebody or demonstrates something everybody watches. And those who knew me couldn't believe that I squatted. They cheered, and Master Wang smiled. I was elated. It was an awesome experience. That was four months ago, and I can still do deep knee bends, and sit right down on my heels!

The thing that I believe is important to know is that it was not a carnival act, and it was not something that really happened spontaneously on Master Wang's part. He had been working on the knee and he knew it would work. But the most amazing part of the whole process is my attitude toward other people and living creatures and the whole thing. But it has happened in such small increments over the past year and a half that I didn't realize that it was happening until one day I just realized, this is different, I really am different.

John is quiet and reflective. The soft breeze ruffles the wind chimes as he wipes away tears. A significant emotional shift has occurred for him during his physical healing process.

As the heart and emotions open up, the more healing seems able to take place. Recently when I was initiated into the eleventh disciple group, boy, at that empowerment ceremony, I was very emotional. Yeah.... You know I was a policeman for 18 or 20 years, and a Marine and all these kind of things, and boys don't cry and stuff. It's a real opening up. I find that seems to be a common occurrence sometimes at the healings, that I do cry. And, at other times....

John wipes away more tears. We sit in silence for awhile to absorb this opening up of spirit and emotion. The wind chimes occasionally break the silence. I finally ask John if he regularly practices any of the Qigong techniques that he has learned from Master Wang.

I do practice, but I have to admit, not as often as I should. I practice at home about three times a week and I go to a group practice twice a month. I usually do Five Elements and One Finger Zen Part One, probably for 20 to 30 minutes each. I intentionally slow down a little bit, because you can really zip through them more quickly. I particularly like One Finger Zen Part One. I just like all the movements, although I feel energy in both of them.

I'd have to say that Qigong has changed my outlook on life. I've had two big changes in my life. The first one was in 1975. I had a heart attack, and after that things changed for me. Because finally you realize that you're fragile. Before that, you can't die, but then you realize you can die. And so that changed me.

And after meeting Master Wang, I've changed a lot more, the same direction, but much more. It's...it's very emotional. I don't know how to explain it. We seem to have a connection. I mean a deep connection. And I haven't completely figured that out. That was why I asked to become a disciple. I have decided that my path is to do whatever he wants, to help him. It's an experience that I just don't know how to tell you.... I don't know what else to say.....My whole life has changed. The thing that I don't understand is that I have no reservations about doing anything that he asks. Normally, you feel intimidated around somebody of his stature and I don't. No questions. I'm normally a very skeptical person but...it just seems right. Every time he says something there's a lesson in it, although sometimes they go over your head and you don't get them the first time. I've never known anyone like Master Wang. He's changed my life.

3 Persistence and Patience

I drive past small clusters of houses in a rural area of Santa Cruz county. Some are neatly maintained, others are haphazardly added onto. Leoma lives in one of these add-ons. I follow her direction, walk around the main house and into the back yard looking for the studio apartment she has described. All I see is a ramp leading to two back doors. I call her name and she opens the door nearest the ramp and invites me in. The door opens into a tiny kitchen with steps leading up to a small platform containing a sleeping bag and under the window, a table crowded with plants.

Leoma finishes her lunch then invites me up to the third level of this tiny abode. A snug loft is hung in a space above the kitchen, four steps up from the sleeping platform. We dodge each other in moving about. She carefully navigates the stairs, expertly avoiding the clothing, shoes, blankets and pillows that line them.

The loft is filled with light from several windows. A mattress blanketed with pillows takes up most of the space, leaving just enough open floor for her to practice Qigong. I make myself comfortable at one end of the mattress. Leoma moves her laptop computer, rearranges a strong reading light on the wall behind her and tucks her feet under a pillow.

I remember the ashen woman I met three and a half years ago at one of Master Wang's first California workshops. It was very difficult for her to stand or navigate and she spent most of the session lying down on a mat. As Leoma leans back now to talk about her illness and her experiences with Qigong and Master Wang, her face glows in the afternoon light.

I guess it's been about 18 or 19 years by now, I can't remember the exact date, although there was a specific time of starting, I'm just not good with dates. It's neurological. It was originally diagnosed as multiple sclerosis, although the neurologist is no longer sure now exactly what it is. I'm not exhibiting the signs that he would expect of going downhill more rapidly. He was already unsure of this before I did Qigong, but I've done a lot of things over the years that he doesn't realize. He just doesn't understand for instance that things like acupuncture make a big difference.

I also have environmental illness which means that I'm exceedingly sensitive to things like carpets and a lot of materials used in housing. The neurological problem means that I have some paralysis in the left leg, some semi-paralysis in the left hand, and bladder and bowel control difficulties. Tiredness. There's also been some difficulty in the back and the spine area.

The most difficult thing is that it's unpredictable. If I extend myself and do too much I'll go into a down period where I have almost no energy and have to rest and recoup for maybe a month. I mean it's gotten to where it's less, but it can take quite awhile to come back. There was a period after my back first got bad where I couldn't be upright for more than about an hour before I would get very tired and trembly and would have to lie down. If I get too tired, I can get really disoriented.

The environmental illness affects my mind and if I am in a situation where I'm exposed, my ability to think and process things can go. If I'm in pretty good shape, at first it acts like I've had an overdose of coffee, but then it crashes. In the worst situations, like when I was exposed to pesticides when the house was being sprayed for termites, it was as if my mind was being pulled apart. So it can have a very severe effect on my thinking processes. And of course after that is the tiredness and such. So those are the two basic things.

I have seen a neurologist for the neurological problems, but I've actually never gone to a western medical doctor for the environmental illness because so far as I know the western medical establishment doesn't understand much of anything about this. The MS diagnosis came from a western doctor with CAT scans and the rest of that.

A few years ago, when the doctor began to wonder what I had, he put me through a number of tests, like renewed CAT scans. He didn't do a spinal on me because that's very intrusive, but originally there was a spinal done. The new CAT scans show that there is definite impairment in the brain, places of lesion or difficulty. I don't know what the technical word for them is. Places where the brain isn't right because there's been damage of some sort. Scarring or nonfunctional areas do show up on the CAT scan. My doctor sees me as being essentially in a steady state. He doesn't understand the fact that if I overdo it, I go into these relapse times. But because I've learned how to rest, usually I have been able to stop before a relapse.

My whole life for the past 18 or so years has been one of learning how to deal with and adapt to this illness so it doesn't have such a severe effect. Up until a couple of years ago I would go in about once a year and say "What's up, what's new on the horizon for MS?" And now that he no longer thinks I have MS, he just says come in if needed. So it's been awhile since I've been in to see him. He did the CAT scans before I intensively started with Master Wang. Since he doesn't even accept that acupuncture is useful, he would never agree that Master Wang has made a difference. That's one reason I don't go in very often. I mean he doesn't even see that any of this other stuff that I'm doing is relevant.

Over the years I've done a lot of work with Feldencrist, which is the best kind of neurological retraining I've found. Plus, I've done a lot of energy work, Reiki, some energy channeling, work with some spiritual groups, work with diet. I've worked to become very sensitive to my state so that I would respond and rest in time to prevent acute relapse. I've also used acupuncture, herbs, vitamins.

I was doing all of that before I saw Master Wang, and still continue those things that seem to help. Except not so much Feldencrist because my teacher moved to Chicago. I think I could use some more body work, so I'll probably look for some hands on work that's complimentary to the Qigong.

I first went to Master Wang in the winter of 1996, I think it was the second workshop. I went to a healing with somebody. Just checking it out. And they were very welcoming. I think the first one I took was One Finger Zen Part One, which included a review of Five Element Stake. A friend of a friend told us about the healing, so we went just to check it out. Word of mouth, and fairly casual too. No great expectations. I was feeling that maybe I needed to do more exercise or movement work so that was part of it. I wanted to do Qigong or Tai Chi or something. But they were so very welcoming that it was easy to come back.

Later that spring I became a disciple with the second group. Something within me said it was a good thing to do, and I don't know why. So it's one of these mysterious processes that's been part of my healing. Where I'm going on sort of an inner guide who says, "do this." Ask me why I'm doing this, I don't really know. I was hesitating because I didn't know that much about him.....here's this Chinese man.....he could barely speak English....I could barely understand what it was all about. But OK, why am I doing this? Well, just because I am. There's some reason. And I'm not a guru hopper either. It was like something in me knew that it was the right thing to try.

Actually I had some hesitations about taking on a teacher because my sister is a Tibetan Buddhist and I had some notions that this was a serious commitment. But nonetheless I went ahead and did it. And when he taught the Six-Syllable Mantra I could really feel the power of that. I think the higher level teachings have always been the most attractive to me. Although I could really feel the energy in the One Finger Zen, I had a harder time with the Five Element Stake. I have a hard time standing because of the left leg. It's difficult to stand for long periods. But I was trying to do it and I did discover that I was being strengthened.

As I've said, I was already experimenting with different kinds of energy healing. And actually after going to that first healing session with Master Wang I can remember feeling kind of strange afterwards. You know it wasn't like the healing pulled me in at first. Instead, I had some strange emotional reactions. Actually, I think it was the practice that drew me in initially more than the healings. I could recognize the power of the practice

The energy of the healing sessions was there, but it was odd. It wasn't clear-cut to me that this was what I needed to heal my body. It's not like when I first went to a Feldencrist session and my body said "yes!" This healing was more subtle. There was some physical change, but it's not like I had this big physical shift all at once. I mean something was going on but I didn't know exactly what it was, or whether it was emotional or physical. So it was the practice that really drew me in. And when we finally learned the Six-Syllable Mantra, that really drew me.

I've taken all the teachings at least twice. I went to all the workshops in Santa Cruz. And lately as I've gotten stronger I've started to go farther. I mean for awhile I didn't go to anything outside of Santa Cruz because driving is so difficult for me. Even being a passenger would have been too exhausting. And to try to go to a workshop in an unknown place and maybe be environmentally sensitive and all that...

When I went to Master Wang's International Qigong Seminar in San Francisco in October 1998, it was another one of those things which at first seemed like it might be too formidable for me. The first thought was no way. But it just kept coming up and it fell into place. And that teaching, Three-Syllable Mantra, was an incredible one for me.

Sometimes during a healing or teaching with Master Wang, there is spiritual work that is going on. After the Three-Syllable teaching, about a month later, I wasn't feeling very strong in the first syllable. Then as I went to healing sessions, the healing sessions opened up that first syllable for me again. So I feel much more connected to it. I've found that the healings with Master Wang help me reconnect with the teachings. There is no question they are generally strengthening for me. When I go to acupuncture the week after a healing, my acupuncturist almost always feels an unusual strength in my energy. Which isn't really mine, it's from Master Wang, but it's invariably there.

So his healings do give me strength and energy. It often takes a number of days before I feel like I'm back with my own energy. I definitely feel like I carry his energy for a number of days after a healing session. I think it's a matter of whether or not my body can absorb it and then use it to heal. There's no question that the Qigong has helped me, the practices in particular. I think the healings with Master Wang are kind of a jump start to the energy that I can continue on with in my practice. I don't actually practice the next day after a healing. It's more like just being with whatever energy he gave me.

I'm glad for the local group practice sessions because I rarely do One Finger Zen or Five Element by myself. My daily Qigong practice is always Three-Syllable Mantra, Dispelling Negative Energy and Six-Syllable Mantra. I was also doing Vajra Yoga every day. I want to start adding Vajra Yoga back in because I think it's an important one. I practice for as long as it feels right energetically. I don't always include meditation in my practice, but I would like to work up to doing that.

The thing about my illness is that I can still overdo it and go down. But now it takes more to pull me down. I've got more strength, and my back is definitely stronger. But it's a slow thing. I believe that the difficulty in my back is neurological. The Qigong has definitely, slowly over time, been the real factor for healing my back. I can tell that my back is incredibly stronger because I'm being upright most of the day now and I wasn't before. It's not like I intend that today I'm going to be upright. It's more like at the end of the day I will realize oh, I was up more. So there is no question in terms of general stamina it feels like I am tapping into some energy through the practice of Qigong.

I don't expect quick results. There are different ways that things can be healed. One way is you give the body a place where you can nurture yourself and it will return to a state of health. I feel the kind of illnesses I have broke the pattern of health in my body. And in order to find a way out of it, something else must bring in a different pattern. Of course relaxing, nurturing and doing all these other things can help. But in order to really heal it, something new must come in. And this is where I feel the Qigong has really been helping me. It's bringing in a different energy although I actually make the healing possible by continuing to do the practice.

In terms of the environmental stuff, I haven't really worked with trying to use the Qigong specifically for that. When I get stronger I may actually do something like expose myself to a place I know is not good and do some Qigong in it. I'm waiting for the neurological and the general stamina to be more predictable and more easily recouped before I attempt that.

I'm still quite wobbly standing up. So I will need to go back and pick up the One Finger Zen Part One for stability at some point. I would have to do it just standing and thinking about the squatting positions because I'm not ready to squat yet, but I think that practice would help my stability. I need to go slowly and add things bit by bit as they become more appropriate for me.

It can be very hard for me to start a practice. Sometimes I have to work with myself about an hour to get myself upstairs to do it. You talk about challenges. Sometimes there's a real resistance to entering the different energy states and levels, so I have to keep at that until I finally start.

Sometimes I feel inhibited by the sound when I do the mantra practices. But I've just decided that if the people next door have a baby and a two year old that cry, they can listen to mantra. And I'm sure it's good for the little ones. At least I'm not in an apartment building with people on all sides.

Another challenge is that I like to practice up here in this little loft section, because it's a little more removed. This loft space gets very hot in the summer and very cold in the winter. Unbearably hot in the afternoons when the sun comes over, which means that in the summer I have to remember to shift my time of practice.

I feel I'm slowly learning to tap into energy healing. Master Wang says that the Three-Syllable Mantra is supposed to allow us start bringing in our personal energy. The Dispelling Negative Energy practice is also becoming powerful for me. Repeating the teaching does make a difference. I was doing the Dispelling practice before, but the last time I took it from him, I got it on a different level. I finally am getting it so that it's more and more making a difference.

I don't know if the Qigong helps prevent colds or flu. I don't have a sense of that or about my overall resistance. Although sometimes when I've had colds or flu, I do feel the Qigong has helped me heal more quickly. But the main thing is my ability to be upright much longer, and that I am learning to call on energy to heal myself. That's what is really important. Also if I have a relapse, I think it helps speed up recovery. My limits do seem to be farther. I can do more before I crash.

I'd also like to reiterate that for me the daily practice has been the key. Although healings are nice they don't allow me to heal myself. For Master Wang to heal me, what good does it do? I have the sort of illness that recurs. I'm healed, then something else happens and I have to go back again, and again, unless I can heal myself. I remember him talking sometimes about how people call from China in the middle of the night saying, "I need help." I feel that I'd not be a good disciple if I didn't take some responsibility for healing myself.

It's very scary to think about appearing to be better and then crashing so that I go way back. So I'm really interested in the step by step process of healing. The slow process. Little ups and downs are to be expected, but I really want to be solid with it. And I do find that my health has improved with this practice over time.

My experiences with Master Wang have been very interesting...and fruitful. I find it a very hard thing to summarize. The thing is that what is happening, the important things, are really not on the thinking level. They're at a much deeper place. I appreciate the spiritual levels of this practice. As I said, my sister is a Tibetan Buddhist, so I do have some information that I have absorbed from her. One thing my sister has given to me about Tibetan Buddhism is the knowledge that this is a deep and serious practice. Therefore, you don't just play around with it and change it and whimsically do this and that, you really honor the teaching.

I also do some other spiritual practices. Subud, I'm a Quaker. The thing is, Qigong has challenged me to deepen the other things I'm doing. If it were done on a casual or shallow level there might be conflicting energy. But if you can go deeper, then the energy is universal. Each time I learn a higher practice it challenges me to deepen other things. It's been a potent force in my spiritual development as well as in my healing.

4 Karmic Connections

Coastal fog hangs over a wooded hill. Just over the crest, I turn up a private road bordered by tall redwoods. The fog gives way to patchy sunshine and then suddenly a neat one-story house appears in a light filled clearing. Brooke, a gentle woman with a warm smile and graying hair, opens the door when I knock. Her husband, Court, lounges on the sofa. He is pale. Color is just beginning to come back into his normally ruddy face after a recent bout with pneumonia, His faithful Molly, a border collie mix, is spread out protectively at his feet. Although I am here to interview both Court and Brooke, I choose to interview Court first in order to conserve his limited energy.

I'm going to deal with two different sets here, the most important one being my coming down with chronic fatigue immune system dysfunction syndrome called CFIDS. It's a disease that is now on the list of those diseases that the Center for Disease Control in Atlanta says is number one on the rise in the United States, and there is no known cure. It's extraordinarily debilitating. They have a nickname for it, they call it the "living death." And that's a pretty apt description. At its worst, your cognitive functions are completely gone. Your memory is completely gone. Your body is fibromyalgic. In other words it feels like you're arthritic throughout. You have no energy whatsoever and no capacity to do anything. And many people are for years bedridden.

I connected up with this disease process in around 1992. It really left me in a place where I was half dead, and the depression that goes with it is sufficient that you really don't care if you're here or not. Leaving was just as good an option as staying. But I did a number of things, and went on quite an odyssey of various therapeutic processes.

That's one disease that I was dealing with as I met Master Wang. Secondly, I was diagnosed as having a blood disease, polycythemia, which is an overabundance of red blood cells—a continual production of red cells where ultimately the blood refuses to flow through your body and that's the end of your script. It's a slow process, a bone marrow disease. You can give someone a lot of comfort by draining a quart of blood or so every month. But as far as a cure, there is no known cure other than a complete bone marrow transplant. Those were the two things that were going on when I met Master Wang.

The polycythemia was diagnosed by western medicine. The chronic fatigue was denied by western medicine. At that time, if you went to most physicians and said, "I've got chronic fatigue," the response would be, "Why don't you go down and see your nearest psychiatrist. I can't see anything wrong with you, nor can I test for it." So they would go into denial around what chronic fatigue would be.

In the last couple of years, it's been recognized as an extremely serious process which is very much on the rise in the U.S. There's a lot of very intense research going on now into what constitutes this particular disease process. I've dealt with several western doctors who have come up to speed on this, but in terms of their having any solid way of being able to handle it, it's probably the same situation as with cancer, the cancer is not cured the majority of time.

The main thrust of what happens is your mind goes, you have no memory. For example, I got this pneumonia bug. I got rid of that and immediately I got whacked again with chronic fatigue. I couldn't even remember the multiplication tables. I mean that's right back where I was with this stuff. Although this time it is starting to unwind rather rapidly so I don't think I'm going to be beset with years of it like I was before I started seeing Master Wang.

Very simply I can tell you what happened. In the first instance I was dealing with polycythemia. This particular variant of polycythemia is supposed to go in only one direction, and that is straight up until such time as you depart. I first saw Master Wang about two years ago, in 1997. I was attending healings every week. After roughly four months of being with him the red blood count started to taper off and head back toward normal. My hematologist watched this and said, "You know this just doesn't happen. The blood just does not go back to normal with this variant of polycythemia that you have." And when I got back to normal, he just looked at me and said, "Score one for Master Wang." My polycythemia returned only once, briefly, then went back into remission and it has remained in remission ever since.

Now let's take a look at the second piece. We're talking about chronic fatigue and it's an entirely different animal. At first, I didn't really get a sense that I was making too much progress with Master Wang around chronic fatigue. Every afternoon I would get a little fever and I'd start to feel myself go. My energy would drop, my mind would go off-line and I'd turn into a vegetable. It's really a dreadful process because the depression that goes with it is just awesome. And the insomnia was equally discouraging.

But when Master Wang gave an empowerment ceremony up in San Francisco last year, I went in there feeling OK. Not up or down, just OK. I walked in there and four hours later I had a fever of 105 and I started to hallucinate. I couldn't move my limbs. Brooke rolled me into the emergency room. They didn't know what the hell was wrong with me. They did what they could do, but they were pretty concerned. You know a guy 70 years old with 105 degree fever is not a good deal as far as they're concerned.

Brooke leans forward to interject: You probably did have a degree or two going into that, but the fact is that the energy really pushed it up. It just skyrocketed after he got touched on the head with the special implement during the empowerment. By the time we got home his muscles had just melted and he couldn't stand up at all. Even though I knew that Master Wang talked about fevers as healing, it was much too scary to handle so we went to the ER. I don't even know what they did. They took all kinds of tests and nothing showed up. But within a day or two after the empowerment Court was all taken care of. I think that he moved up to another level of health. We told Master Wang about it later and he said that Court probably would not have survived without that fever. So it was really important.

Court: Yeah, the funny thing about it is that I never had fevers again. And I have not had them since. So something, some pretty pernicious pathogens, got nailed with that fever, and it was within an inch of nailing me too.

Brooke: I just want to add something in, because I know that you feel that Master Wang didn't do as much for the chronic fatigue. The thing I want to add is that in my experience over the year and a half before that, as we were working with him, your energy did keep racheting up. You did keep getting healthier even though you would go through a lot of illness along the way. At first you would be totally wiped out for days after seeing Master Wang. Now you've gotten where you can go to a healing and you can keep on functioning afterwards.

Court: Yes. That's a very good point. That first year I would go to Master Wang with a great deal of trepidation because I knew there was going to be three days of hell afterward. And it was absolutely deathly. I would say OK I'm going to do this, but I'd have to really rev myself up in order to go and do the work with Master Wang.

Brooke: I certainly think that the reason Court's still around is because he got so much energy from Master Wang. We feel that Court is still sitting here today because we found Master Wang. We met him through doing some other Qigong. We got the flyers for his healings and workshops for a long time, but I don't think I showed them to Court. I knew that I couldn't even get myself to a Yoga class much less take on another practice. I thought what's the sense in even exposing myself if I'm not going to follow through on it. It wasn't until Court was desperately ill one day that I thought well let's just go try this, and we went. The first time we went in, Master Wang recognized Court.

Court: Well, the translator came over and said that Master Wang told her to tell me that I had been assigned to him someplace in Tibet. And that's not in any variance with an awful lot of other experiences that I've had with various people within the Tibetan lineage. I became a very good friend of Sogyal Rinpoche and flew him around the countryside. And I got a call one time asking if I'd be interested in personally flying the Dali Lama from Santa Ana up to Watsonville, which I did. But I feel a certain closeness to Master Wang that I can't quite describe to you.

Most of the time in the healing sessions, I totally disappear. There's no Court. I have no thoughts, no me. You know, whoever walked in there as Court is long gone. Very seldom do I have any awareness of anything. Immediately after the healings I would feel fine. Then the next day the roof would fall in. But that's not true now. If I walked in and had a healing with Master Wang today, I would expect to be able to walk out of there and not expect that the next day would be a disaster.

I have attended some of the workshops. Enough that I can do aspects of Five Elements, Six Syllable Mantra, Three Syllable Mantra, One Finger Zen. I try to get some practice in every day but I can only do about 12 to 15 minutes. That's not very long. But I have seen a correlation between the practice and my healing. Physical, spiritual and emotional healing. All of these have been addressed.

Overall, Master Wang has had a profound effect on my health. He is more than a high level Tibetan Buddhist Qigong master. I see him, I experience him as a very high level being irrespective of whatever his lineage happens to be. So around Master Wang I feel like I am in the presence of someone who is beyond presence. He is much more to me than a very skilled Qigong master or a high level Nyingma lineage holder. I know he's a lot more than I see him as being.

I became a disciple of the ninth group. It was a fine experience for me to do that. I see Master Wang when I come to healings, and we always have a greeting. It lifts my heart to be with him. And I know I've come a long way.

Court is obviously tired from talking so I shift the interview to Brooke. There is something reticent, very subdued about her. It may be the years of caregiving, or perhaps because in spite of his illness, Court is a forceful person who commands attention. As she begins her story, I notice that Brooke's eyes are the color of sky. I also notice that she seems much more relaxed than when I first met

her almost two years ago. The worry lines around her mouth have
eased, and her infectious laugh bursts out more often.

I have low energy and emotionally it was very
difficult for me with Court being so ill. Court and I had
a very challenging relationship as it was. So with all of
that together I was under a lot of strain a lot of the
time. I primarily went to Master Wang at a point where
we were very desperate to find something, because in
spite of all of our many resources Court wasn't getting
any better. That's why I showed up there, mainly
because of Court's illness, not because of my own
problems. But you know after the first healing I was
perfectly happy to go back! I loved those healings. I
wouldn't be conscious of what was going on in the
room, but at the end when I would come back, I would
just be filled with such sweetness. And it was so
wonderful to feel like somebody was taking care of me.
You know I was working so hard all the time, putting
out and putting out and putting out. And to have that,
to feel the blessing of that healing energy and know
that I could sit there and relax and be filled with this
sweetness—I was won over at the first healing.

Master Wang once did a house clearing for us.
Pretty early on we asked for private healings. Somehow
or another he was willing to come here to the house
to do the healings although he didn't normally do that.
I have a feeling it was because he knew that it was
something with the house itself that was causing or
adding to Court's difficulty. So he came here twice to
do small group healings.

I don't remember if it was the first or the
second time. The two blend together a little. At one

point he had us sitting outside in the sunshine. Our eyes were closed. Suddenly we heard our dog Molly tearing down the driveway barking her head off. I thought what is she up to now! Master Wang told us later that at that very moment he had expelled the negative entities out of our house. Molly saw them and she was chasing after them, nipping at their heels.

He's very careful about what he says about things like that. He said that there were negative entities in the house that were suppressing Court's ability to heal, so he must have thought that it was very important to do that in order for him to do anything else for Court.

Master Wang also played a big part in our relationship. We were having tremendous difficulties. At one point we were ready to split up, and he basically said that there would be terrible karmic consequences if we did. Then he worked with us and said that it should get better. And it didn't get better. But I still have to give Master Wang some of the credit because without his work we might not have gotten to the point of seeing a therapist. Therapy is not what Master Wang does, but he had a lot to do with the way that process unfolded even though there were certain things that we had to uncover in a very western way. I felt like he was praying for us and we could definitely feel his blessings and concern. So I would be willing to say that things have changed internally, partly because of that energy as well as us doing the work.

Dispelling Negative Energy was the first workshop I went to and I didn't know anything. But I felt that our connection to Master Wang was so important.

I was really both struck and touched that Master Wang was giving so much personal attention to Court that I wanted to do everything I could to build that connection. That first workshop, I went more to show respect than because I was thinking we would actually take up a Qigong practice. It took us at least a year of working with Master Wang before we even started doing the practices ourselves. Because we were just in such desperate need to have energy coming in. It was a long time before we had enough energy funded inside of us to move into doing the practice ourselves.

I do additional practices now beyond what Court does. I have more energy to do the practice than Court does. All my life I've carried a lot of tension in my muscles. I've found that if I've not gotten much exercise during the day or if I've been really busy and I do Five Elements at night, my body goes through lots of shaking off. My body moves all over the place and I think OK, I've gotten my exercise. I released all of this stuff and I can go to bed and sleep really well. So there are times like that when I might go and do more.

I myself have never had a particular physical problem I could identify. Yet, its very clear to me that receiving that much blessing and that much energy from Master Wang really helped me spiritually and emotionally, and I'm sure also helped me physically. Certainly since I've been doing the Qigong practice myself I feel better than I have in years. It's really noticeable. It's a major contribution in terms of how my energy has shifted. The spiritual blessings have been very important. Master Wang has been a really crucial person in our lives.

5 | A Spiritual Path

*Akin is raking leaves as I approach his home in
a wooded suburb near Monterey. I cross a wooden
bridge and he welcomes me warmly into his
home, tucked across a creek amid a stand of oaks.
We take off our shoes in the entryway. Rice paper
on the windows filters the afternoon light. I follow
him into a room filled with Asian furnishings:
Chinese palace chairs, a massive gold and black
screen, pillows on the floor.*

*Akin's home reflects his temperament:
comfortable, thoughtful, articulate. Classical music
and a fire warm the living room on this cool fall
day. The focal point of the room is a carved
wooden altar with several Buddhas in niches. I
notice the Tibetan mala (prayer beads) he wears on
his wrist as he reaches to show me a very special
carved Buddha given to him by a teacher in
Nepal. I turn it in my hands and I can feel its
energy.*

*I sink into the cushioned sofa as Akin
begins his story. A gentle man with light chocolate
skin and a neat white beard, he punctuates his*

*conversation with long slender fingers. His voice is soft but
confident. Sitting across from him on the sofa I am aware that I
am in the presence of a spiritual being.*

I was diagnosed HIV positive in 1985, although I
suspect that I acquired the virus in the late 70's. During
that time, of course, there was no official name for it. I
had just noticed that friends were dying of this
extremely rare illness. It was primarily linked, at that
time, to gay men. Within that context, I decided that I
would not have any relationships because I was afraid.
That's why I think I acquired it in the late 70's because
I had no relationships after that.

And so by 1985 the only test came out. I took it
and I was positive. It was devastating for me. In effect,
I went into denial and decided that there was no cure,
so I was on my path to die. It was real heavy. There was
shame and guilt. It's interesting because I always had
been raised as a "good kid." I had done well in school, I
had gone on to the university. I received my graduate
degree in architecture from UC Berkeley. At that point I
had even been a university professor. So for something
like this to happen was very devastating. I didn't tell my
family. I told virtually no friends. I saw two therapists
shortly after my diagnosis. I shared my diagnosis with
them and told no one else.

It was very hard...I think back....well, it was
seven years later I became ill. But from 1985 to 1992
was a very terrible time in my life. I would not like to
see anyone have to go through that. That's why as part
of my work that I do now with the AIDS Project, I
encourage people who test positive to seek out

support from their community, and if possible from family. Family is not always there for one, but seek out friends. Make your own family.

So my path starts for me, my spiritual life actually began in 1992, after falling ill in August and nearly dying. I was still in denial of having HIV. I had caught a cold or something and I thought it was a typical kind of cold. You know the kind that lasts for a week or so and you get over, but it sort of lingered. I didn't make a connection to my HIV, but at a certain point I was taken into the emergency room of the hospital. I was near death. My body was in effect shutting down.

I was undergoing renal failure, congestive heart failure. I had a viral pneumonia with a complication that was called empyema. It was a fluid that gathered between my skin and my lung sac and it was a source of infection and could have killed me. When I was admitted to the hospital they found that there were so many complications. After I admitted that I had tested HIV positive they did the antibody test and found that I had a very low T-cell count. They were of the opinion that I was too ill to revive so they were going to ship me off to Hospice to die.

Fortunately, I would say the first angel came into my life, my doctor. An immunologist with Community Hospital of Monterey, she was one of the first physicians in the area to establish an AIDS clinic and AIDS unit in the hospital. She returned from vacation and read my file within a few days of my going into the hospital. She decided I had a series of complications that she felt could be cured. So I remained in the hospital for 45 days, and during that 45 days I was treated with some very powerful antibiotics. It was a very aggressive regimen, but it was what I needed to bring me through.

During this same time, I had occasion to meet a Catholic priest who had also been instrumental in establishing the AIDS agency here. So he began to work with me and help me along the spiritual path. One of the first things I can recall when I was admitted to the hospital, that evening, one of the physicians came in and had a frank talk with me. He said that I was extremely ill with numerous complications and that I would have to bring forth my faith or spirituality to help them heal me. He told me they were going to do the best they could but that I was very weak with a lot of medical problems. He said it's going to take teamwork, you're going to have to want to heal yourself. And so I decided in the hospital that night that I was going to become a part of my own survival. And I took an attitude of I'm going to work toward healing, and that life is worth living. It's interesting, I have journeyed with some other people who have died from AIDS and there's a certain point of giving up. But I took the stance that I find life to be rewarding. I wanted to continue to interact with others, with nature, with the universe and to continue to learn about things.

I decided to be pro-active. And that's what I did. So during that 45 days I learned all I could about hospitals. They would come in to do my vital signs and I kept a little notebook. I later heard one of the nurses say that it was a wonderful coping device for my having been there so long. It enabled me to have something to do. Like when they came in to take my temperature, my pulse, they were charting. But I would ask them what the reading was so I could do my own charting and I could keep up with things and I could involve myself. I could look at my charting and see if over a period of time my temperature was going down, if certain medications seemed to be working or not, and so it was a good process.

Four years after this episode I first saw Master Wang. It was at his first healing session at Land of Medicine Buddha (LMB) in Soquel in 1996. I have memories of that event because I had gone up to LMB on several occasions before and I saw a flyer announcing the Qigong healing and workshop, and I thought, oh, this sounds very interesting. There was a little passage about Master Wang and I thought, this is something I must come up to do.

I had already made my first journey to Nepal. When I went to Nepal I took refuge into Tibetan Buddhism and that's what enabled me to find LMB. I was looking for a Dharma center in California that would be close to where I could do my practice. So I had already taken refuge when I first met Master Wang.

I was rather stable at the time, but I was beginning to experience another complication, gout, as the result of my weakened kidneys. I had experienced it once before. And when I went up to the weekend workshop with Master Wang, it came about again. That weekend was a very special time for me. I really got the sense and the benefit of Master Wang's healing energy because he identified the pain that I was having and assisted me with relieving the pain of the gout. That is a testament of my respect for him and also my feeling that he is a healer and someone with whom I would like to work.

My goal is to continue to heal myself as I go through this challenge, but I would also like to be able to master the energy so that I can help others. It's interesting, I can't use the word cure because it just seems so complex. But there's a level of healing that I think I can achieve for my own stability. And then to have this ability to go a little farther and heal others is another goal.

When I went to that first workshop I really felt the energy, and I felt the healing that came through, and the compassion and the warmth of Master Wang as well. On my first trip to Nepal I stayed at a monastery outside Katmandu for a period of time. I encountered the lamas there and it was interesting because I was very uncomfortable with them. I saw these men who were so enlightened and so spiritually at ease. I went through a process of having such a profound respect for them that I wasn't comfortable around them. It wasn't about being afraid of them, but just not knowing how to act properly. Fortunately I had the chance in Nepal to go partially through that process with spiritual beings. So when I met Master Wang I saw the same thing that I had experienced in Nepal with the spiritual leaders there, but I felt very comfortable with him. There's something about evolved beings such as Master Wang that conveys compassion and humility and other qualities that we are not quite accustomed to in our culture. In our western culture we're more used to competitiveness and aggressiveness and ego and all those things.

In the past four years I have attended six to eight workshops and a number of healing sessions. One Finger Zen Part One and Two, Five Element Stake, Six Syllable Mantra, Patting the Meridians. I have also attended a few repeats. It's rare that you can get all the techniques down in one workshop so attending repeat workshops is an opportunity to refine the practice and to gather more energy.

During the healing sessions there are several sensations that I feel, and they have changed or evolved in different ways in the last few sessions. They have gotten more intense. But generally I feel a sense of warmth coming over my body. I can feel energy when it's directed to me, and I have spontaneous movement that's usually just a mild shaking. My arms will shake and my legs will shake and I will just go into a period of shaking. Relaxation. You could call it that. You know, it's shaking but not jolting or anything. And I will do that for a period of time. I've experienced colors of purple and gold and blue during the sessions.

What I usually find is that time seems to speed up, because in the normal two and a half hour session when Master Wang announces that the session is over it seems like it's only been half an hour. I've never been correct in guessing or feeling the full length of time. Time just suspends and evolves somehow. It never appears as long as it is. It never appears that it's two or two and a half hours. It always seems like just half an hour. It's always a surprise that it's time to open your eyes.

My health is generally better after a healing. I've

given Master Wang charts of my lab work, although trying to make a correlation has taken me a little time because sometimes when I've had a healing session with Master Wang I may not have lab work for another week or so, or I may have had lab work the week before. But what I've sensed and what I feel is that his sessions have been extremely healing for me. As he's described it, his efforts are to cleanse the toxins from my kidneys, my liver and my spleen. So in doing that he is helping to heal me. By cleansing the toxins, forcing them through my system, down through my extremities, he cleanses my organs and that helps my body to regenerate and continue to heal.

The wonderful thing is that Master Wang not only cleanses the toxins from my HIV, but also from the medications that I take. Over a period of time I've taken a number of medications, and many of them are very toxic. At one time I was taking as many as eight medications, which came to about 24 or 25 pills a day. Currently, I take maybe 17 pills a day.

I've gone through periods where I've made a decision not to go with western medicine. I've gone with eastern medicine, Chinese herbs. I've always included acupuncture and massage and meditation into my health regimen. I've used complimentary medicines, as I would call them, in combination with western medicines. And only after I did a lot of reading did I agree to go back and start using western medicines because they were finally beginning to show some good results. I attribute my health now to a combination. My healing practice is that I take the best of all forms.

My doctor knows about all these other things I'm doing and she feels that they are complementing what she's doing. In fact I described to her what my plan is in terms of my healing, like the healing sessions, etc. I don't go into detail with her in terms of the practice, but I've told her that I'm studying ways to balance the qi in my body, to bring the qi from the universe into my body in order to heal and to cleanse and purify the organs. And I not only go to healing sessions with Master Wang, but I also do the practices I've learned from him to heal myself. My doctor finds that to be totally agreeable.

I would say one thing that helped to convince her was that when I first went to Nepal, I had 12 or 15 T-cells. I had seen the film *Little Buddha* a year or so prior to that and I saw this building which happens to be the stupa in Bodinan and it was fascinating. At the top it has the eyes of Lord Buddha which watches over the city. I saw this piece of architecture and I said, I must go there. I must go there to see that. And within about six months I heard about a small tour group that was going, with a friend who lives here. And I thought, wow, this is a coincidence, I'm going to see if I can make my way there. So trying to piece everything together I was able to go with that group.

It was interesting, because with 15 T-cells, you're taking a big risk to go all the way off to Asia for three weeks. It was planned as a three-week trip with an additional two and a half weeks to stay at the monastery if you wanted. So I said, I want to go, I need to go. It put the doctor in an interesting situation, because on the one hand they may say that this is not safe for you to go. But then again, this may well be your very last trip, so why not go.

So my doctor gave me a thorough exam, and I was as healthy as I could have been at that point. But I went there and I survived. In fact I had done so well that after the three weeks, I decided to stay on. The purpose of the trip was to go to Nepal to study Hinduism and Buddhism in Katmandu Valley. It was a wonderful trip. Our guide had lived in Nepal for three years and she had taken refuge as a Tibetan Buddhist. But she was also very interested in Hinduism so she was able to give us a wonderful survey of Katmandu Valley and the spiritual practices we encountered there.

Afterwards, I stayed on for the additional two weeks to attend a 10-day meditation course at Copan Monastery. That's when I went in depth into aspects of Tibetan Buddhism in the philosophical and historical sense and began the practice. It happened that we were there during the Tibetan New Year, so I was also able to experience the celebrations for the festivals and so forth, and it was all connected. I must say that I became spiritually awakened during this time because every question I had about life, about after life, about death, fear of death, my relationship with the universe, and the universal spirit, compassion—all those questions were answered.

It was a very rich experience. I stayed for the entire time. My friend that went with me wanted to stay on even longer and trek. I was at the point where I told him that I no longer had any fear, any fear of death or anything. I told him that I would be able to make the 24-hour journey home by myself. It was a very big shift, because originally I had the assurance of having two friends in the group. We had mapped out a plan that if I were to get ill, I would first check into the Hilton, because they always have western doctors there, and that in a few days if there were something major I would go off to Sydney, Australia. That was the closest place that would have a western AIDS facility. It was really planned out. The evacuation plan was very good on several levels. It also allowed me to rest and enjoy the trip because I knew there was a way I could be taken care of if something were to happen.

So when I came back to California I went to a Catholic retreat center on the Big Sur coast. I needed a place for my transition. So I came back and I drove down there for three days and did my transition. Within a few days after that I went in for a physical exam with my physician. She was amazed, totally amazed. All my tests were even better than when I left. She saw this total change in me. She saw a spiritual quality that she couldn't really quantify on paper, but she could see this real evolution. She found it so amazing that I could come back from a tough trip like that and be so much better.

I continue to have a daily practice for meditation. My Qigong varies. I switch between Five Element Stake and One Finger Zen. I'm very interested in One Finger Zen Part One since I've taken it again. Part Two is always good for the stability and the energy I get. I have had a few lapses in my consistent practice because of time. That's what happens here in the west. But I attribute the meditation, the practice, the spiritual belief and the healings of Master Wang, and the practices of my other teachers as being a major source of my stability. I sent in my paperwork to become a disciple. The last initiation that Master Wang gave I wasn't able to be there, but I do eventually hope to become a disciple.

Time has been my major challenge to doing the practice. I've benefited because I've also been a part of the Qigong practice group in Carmel. We've had a weekly practice for at least two years. I always do the weekly practice unless I'm traveling. We feel the energy grow as a group. We share energy. The group varies from six to nine people normally. The weekly practice is like a sangha (a Buddhist community), and I really look forward to it.

By feeling the power and the energy of Qigong, I would say the greatest benefit for me has been the cleansing and the purification of my body as I proceed through this illness. With Acquired Immune Deficiency Syndrome, as they call it, the virus continues to duplicate. By impacting the immune system, it gradually defeats the immune system. So if I can have a way to cleanse toxins out of my body that allows my immune system to have to fight a little less, it gives me more time.

It provides me more time, I would say, in the part of me that sees life and has the will to live in terms of being a part of the universe in this present form. You know, in looking at my Buddhist philosophy, the notion that this body is just a vessel, and that the real life is contained in that which we might call spirit or self, the focus on this form becomes somewhat of an attachment. And as we really focus on this form, this body, this existence as the beginning and end, it doesn't make any sense.

Whereas in my philosophical nature, at one point I said if I were able to achieve enlightenment in eight lifetimes that would be an adequate goal for myself. But in studying with Master Wang, I find that in the Nyingma school of Tibetan Buddhism, there's the possibility of achieving enlightenment, or rainbow body, in one lifetime. So now I'm in the process of making that philosophical transition. I had originally taken refuge in the Mahayana school, and in that philosophy generally what I have ascribed to is that I would continue to be reborn until all sentient beings are free from suffering. Whereas in the Tantric process of the Nyingma school, I may be able to achieve rainbow body in one lifetime. And I find that to be very interesting because both schools tell us that we are able to develop an awareness that empowers us to know the point of transition from this life. I'm looking at a situation where perhaps when it's time for me to make the transition from this body I will hopefully be able to apply the principles of what I've learned in Qigong to achieve rainbow body, or to come back and be reborn in my own tradition. So that's where I am now. That's why I've waited a bit to become a disciple. I've had to make the shift in philosophy from the Mahayana school to the Nyingma. But I'm pretty clear now that the Nyingma tradition of Master Wang is going to be the path I would like to take.

I never expected to go back to work. Again, a combination of spiritual practice and western medicines, and I would say the supportive nurturing of a family of friends have enabled me to work again. After my illness in 1992, after my 45 days in the hospital, I still had about three months of recovery because I had chest tubes and so forth. And then it was a slow process of being able to move around and walk again. There was a process of about three to four years of building back up in order to feel a sense of being normal. And then it was OK I'm stabilized just enough to go on with life and just be here. But I never thought I'd be able to step into the next category as I've done recently of agreeing to take a position with the Monterey County AIDS Project on a full time basis.

My experience of living with AIDS has a certain value in terms of working with people coming into our office whether they are living with AIDS or coming in for testing or whatever. So my experience is there. Since I'm surrounded by non-Buddhists for the most part, I don't discuss my Buddhist philosophy much but I try to live it. The idea of living by example. People will say, you seem calm and you seem not to be judgmental. So instead of preaching, I'm living it. It opens the door. That's where I find my practice works. It's by living it, and not so much intellectualizing or discussing it with people who are not Buddhists.

The challenges are always here for us. Sometimes I think if I had not acquired AIDS, where would I be? Many times I'm saddened because I do have the virus, but at the same time I've seen so many things that have been so positive for me in terms of my spiritual path. And it's actually set me on the spiritual path.

For instance when I went to Nepal and I went to the monastery, after a few days I wanted to talk about myself. So I told my teacher the nun and I told the lama, the Abbot of the monastery, who was also my teacher, about my having AIDS. And their reaction was, you know we're not judging you. In the Buddhist sense of nonjudgment, all we can say is that we're very sorry that you have a complication, but you can look at this as an opportunity for you to practice compassion, to go inside and learn and understand about yourself and your spiritual path. I never had heard this here in the west. That's a big shift, and so very supportive.

To sum up my experience with Master Wang, I would say that I like his compassion and his skill. His mastery of Qigong is awesome. It's interesting, as he's learned English and is talking to us more directly, he's becoming my teacher. He's more to me than just my teacher for the practice of Qigong. He's becoming my teacher for life and for life's journey. Because in his teachings he's talking about compassion and his own life experiences, the challenges he's had in life. I admire him for that. In fact, I learn something new every time from him. It's so different from what I've learned in the west. For instance, he said in the last session that he would like for his students to surpass him in developing skills for Qigong. The knowledge is so important that he would like for it to be continued. You don't find very many teachers who want their students to surpass them. With most teachers, you're always going to be a student, there's always a separation. It's very unusual. He's a good father, a wonderful father.

I've always admired Master Wang, from when I first met him. I recognize his energy and what he has to give. And I'm very grateful that he's come to the west to share this teaching with us, not only to carry on the tradition but also as a valid means of human expression. It's like caring for the body and caring for the soul. For those of us here in the west who experience this Qigong teaching it is a way to better ourselves and to better function in this world.

6 Visions of Healing

I pass an encroaching tract of estate style homes in the foothills north of Santa Rosa, then turn into a long uphill driveway that leads to a locked gate. Aiea waves to me from the porch of a mobile home up the hill and hurries down to open the gate. We introduce ourselves. Her tanned face crinkles into a warm smile that belies the facts of her illness. Aiea's home looks out onto an organic vineyard and a valley that shimmers with the golden grasses of Indian summer. Oak laced hills frame the distance. She tells me there are geese and deer on these four acres.

She's just moved to this spot, but Aiea's simply furnished home is already neat, the walls already hung with her art, icons of healing. On her altar is a large statue of Qyan Yin. Outside, a priority has been the building of a pond with carp and frogs hiding under lily pads. The pond is a central theme of the ecology oriented children's stories she plans to write. In the cool shade of oaks a serene Buddha keeps watch over the cats. There is a white cat with skin cancer. Aiea has told him he must stay in the shade, which he mostly does.

The morning is already warm, but a slight breeze billows a lace curtain hung across the doorway. We sit at the kitchen table. Aiea has introduced me to her parrot who climbs on an elaborate perch near the front door. Usually talkative, he is suddenly mute in my presence. He listens intently as she begins her story.

I was a full time student going for my BA degree at Sonoma State. A lump appeared on my neck and I became very tired. This was five years ago. I went through the school clinic and they thought it was all these other things. No one for a moment thought it was cancer. And I did. I intuitively knew I had cancer. I kept saying, I have cancer, and they kept saying, you don't have that. A month before finals I had to go in for surgery to get the lump out. And it was cancer, lymphoma. Small cell lymphoma. They feel that I had it for at least six or seven years because it was in so many places in my body. Before the surgery they did a whole range of tests. But the surgery confirmed it was lymphoma.

So I finished the semester, took my finals, with my 4.0, and then took off a semester. I have been a vegetarian for years and a vegan off and on. I have practiced meditation for probably 15 years and Tai Chi, Yoga and movement. So in a way I think I was somewhat prepared to cope with this whole thing. I was actually very relieved with the diagnosis because I felt that I could deal with it. Not knowing, to me, was much worse. I panicked for a bit because this diagnosis is a big, big thing when you love the planet that you live on so much. I am a total nature freak. I love it! And I spend so much of my life and have since I was a child just sitting and being in nature because I just love it.

After the surgery I became so fatigued that I couldn't do anything. I was very, very ill. I was Stage three, quick, within 30 days. They told me horrible things. I was furious that they would dare to cast a death spell on me. They gave me a limited lifespan and told me all these things that were going to happen to my body because I said I was not going to do chemotherapy. Never.

I had this alternative therapist, a really good friend of mine, and he put me on this program of hard core supplements. I tried shark therapy which was horrible. Every time I put it in my mouth all I could think of was that I was eating someone else. It was a horrible experience for me. After three months of that I said I am not this desperate. I cannot eat someone else for me. So I was just very tired and taking all these supplements. It was hard for me to clean my house, it was hard for me to go shopping. Being on disability I couldn't afford anything. I was economically stressed. So this was just a huge impact on my life.

I threw myself heavily into the Yoga. I started trying to stretch out my body so that all this could move out. One of my breasts got really swollen and so sore. That really scared me because I though oh, this is breast cancer too. I went to the place where I was doing Yoga and this woman was there who I had never met before. And this chance meeting is what ultimately led me to Master Wang.

This woman I met at the Yoga place said, "Oh, you have to go in and see a friend of mine, a physician;

and between you and me, she has lymphoma. I work for her and I'll get you in to see her." So she got me an appointment with this doctor who also did herbal therapy. First of all, no one takes Medi-Cal, I mean it's impossible. But this doctor said she'd see me and I got in right away. When I saw this doctor, she said, "I don't want your money. Just forget it. Let's just talk. I'm getting out of practice because working is a real stupid thing to do when you have lymphoma. You should just live. I'm moving and I'm going to live." Then she picked up the phone and called her friend, a doctor who doesn't take any new clients because she's maxed. She asked her as a favor to take me on.

The doctor she referred me to is in fact quite an alternative specialist. She gets calls from all over the United States for help with herbs, and she teaches and such. I was very fatigued and sick when I finally went to see this specialist, about five months after my diagnosis. She was deep and delightful. We talked for an hour and a half. She took my whole story and told me she wanted me to go see a Qigong master in the Bay area, not Master Wang.

Of course I didn't have the money. I went to my Yoga instructor and was talking about it and he gave me the money to go. I had a friend who also had lymphoma. He and I talked and he offered to drive me. This guy is an engineer, straight as they come, not into alternative therapy, but he never did chemotherapy either. He started doing all these other things. And he got me on a rigorous juice diet that I'm still doing today. He's not coming from a spiritual place. His intelligent mind said I'm not going to do western medicine, it'll kill me. So he massively researched all this other stuff and he ended up in the same place I was but from a different direction.

So off we went to see this Qigong master. He is very young, very immature. Later when I met Master Wang I had some great realizations about the differences between them. But he took one look at me and said, "I don't see death on you anywhere, I think we can get you healing." So for two hours he did this private healing, just my friend and I. My friend wasn't there for a healing, but of course he was there getting the energy. I had come there with another lump on my neck, sticking out about an inch. And in that two hours that lump was almost gone. I was sicker than a dog. I was red hot. I couldn't move. I was toxic from head to toe and my friend just threw me in the car. When I got home I was sick for days and the lump was gone. It never came back. Then I slowly began regaining my strength. My friend called all the people in his cancer group and started having this man come out to his house to teach Qigong, and I did that for awhile. But he's very expensive, so I quit going.

I was having some circulation problems but I was gradually getting a little more energy. I was taking some semesters back at school. Only a few classes, about six units. I went to an acupuncturist in town and she referred me to Master Wang. She had also been to this young Qigong master and she told me I would find a really big difference with Master Wang. And I certainly did.

The first time I went to see Master Wang was probably two years ago. I went to one of the group healings in this area. The first time I went my body just totally freaked out. I had violent feelings, I got very hallucinogenic. I felt like I had to vomit and not stop vomiting tumors. I wanted to flop out of my chair and onto the floor and vomit out tumors. But I couldn't do that. I know he says do what you feel like doing. But that was a little extreme. So instead I visualized vomiting tumors for like an hour. Afterward, I was sick for days, but I started to feel my energy return in a really dramatic way. So the next time he was here I went to another healing. I have had candida for years, raging candida, and after that second healing, the candida was gone. And my doctor noticed these changes.

I'm broke, so I could only go to the group healings. Altogether I've gone to seven or eight. I started having a series of visions after the second one. It's incredible. For three days after a healing, always, I'm sick. For three days my body is ill. The vision usually happens between the third to seventh day after the healing. In these visions Master Wang would come to my third eye. This happened three times in a row. He would stand in my third eye and be doing whatever it is he does during a healing, just moving around, walking around and healing me.

Also, immediately after the first healing, I got mantras from nowhere, somewhere, everywhere. And the first one said "I'm going to try to heal." Then it changed to "I'm healing," then to "I'm going to heal." The mantra kept coming in about 20 to 30 minutes during and after the healing. And later when I was having the third eye vision thing I was back in school. I could be sitting in class, in the store, shopping, driving or anything, and Master Wang would pop right in and start doing Qigong.

Then the deeper visions started coming. About 10 days after the fifth or sixth healing I had a major vision. I experienced a remarkable shift during that healing, in body, feelings, everything. In the vision, Master Wang came as a white crane to my third eye. He did this exquisite dance of fingertips which would change from fingertips to feathertips, up high and sweeping low. And he would sweep me, sweep me, sweep me. Then he turned and said, "You can stop worrying now because I'm healing you. You don't have to worry any more. I want you to get up right now and write this down, write this whole vision down." And I got up and wrote the whole thing down in my diary word for word, that experience.

The last time I went to a healing I had all kinds of body stuff again. During the healing, suddenly all this energy just shot, white, through me. I always see white when I'm with him, always white. I see other colors for a moment, but it's white always, and it shot all the way up, flew out my head and ended as a crown of white energy sitting on my head with three distinct things that almost look like lotus blossoms. I can still feel that. I have felt it ever since and it has not gone away. When I walked out of that healing....I have never in my life held reverence for another being ever...but at that moment when that crown hit my head I was filled with the deepest, truest knowing of that person, and love. The mantra that came to me in that last healing wells out of me, just comes out of my mouth, "I don't have cancer anymore, I'm well, I don't have cancer anymore." Sitting with my eyes closed in the healing, my body would bow and say, "Thank you Master Wang, I don't have cancer anymore. Thank you Master Wang, I don't have cancer anymore." That went on and on throughout the whole healing, with this energy thing on my head.

Afterwards, the dream came. About 14 days afterwards, this vision. I was in a casino in Reno and I won the lottery, which was a trip for two to Tibet. I was taking as the second person this little boy about nine years old who was going to replace Master Wang. And I was frightened about it because I've had a lot of bleeding, I have a lot of stuff going on. I was really worried about dealing with menstrual bleeding in Tibet and the environment. I didn't know what to bring or how to deal with it. And then all these Tibetan women appeared at the airport and they were fluffing all over me and dressing me, getting me ready, and they said, "Don't worry we'll take care of all of that. It's not a problem. You're coming with us now to Tibet." So the little boy and I and all these women went to Tibet. And I was told to get up and write all this down. So I did.

I've gone from mistrusting my body, being afraid of my body, into completely trusting. I developed this phenomenal trust for Master Wang, so no matter what my body is doing I know that he's totally taking care of me spiritually and physically and I don't have to worry. The last four or five times all I do is go there to a healing and be. I don't have to do anything. Because I know he is taking care of me. I have never, ever felt so nurtured in my life. What a gentle, special man.

Before I went to see Master Wang, my neck was full of nodes. And now you can't even feel any. They're almost gone. My doctor just said to me two visits ago—and she sends lots of people for Qigong—she has never seen anyone have an experience like I'm having with this. She feels I was somehow connected to Master Wang and because of that I've been able to open up and connect in that plane somewhere.

But I have had an episode recently. And it's interesting because a couple of weeks ago I went to a healing in San Francisco. I felt it was real important I go see Master Wang. I was very tired and I wasn't going to go. I forced myself to go. But he wasn't there, the healing was canceled. I was met at the door and told that Master Wang was called back to Tibet to assist his Dharma brothers. I was going to wait and just go to the next one, but that morning I had this sense that, no, you really need to go today, this is really important, it's connected. And he wasn't there.

So last week I went and had a pelvic ultrasound for the bleeding I've been having and we found a big mass. It could be a lymph node, it could be ovarian cancer. I've gone through fear. I don't know. What can you do ultimately. So this is a little side trip. Everybody I see says Aiea you look great. You're going to hang in there until the cure comes for your kind of cancer. I absolutely feel Master Wang is with me.

When people have an illness like this, commitment to doing the practice yourself is really hard. I do Qigong every day. I gather energy, the Three Palms, and Dispelling. That's about it. That's enough. I really feel it. About 15 minutes. Then if I do it later in the day however long, the magic takes me, I go away. I meditate all day. I don't sit because my body can't, it never could.

The main thing is when you have cancer you lose your energy. It's a level of fatigue that hits you spiritually, physically and emotionally. It's a real exhaustion. In spite of that fatigue you have to find the soul that rises and says get up now and go do Qigong. That's the challenge. Once the body gets up and does three moves, that's it. It's happening, the energy begins to flow.

I feel that Qigong has healed my soul to a place of acceptance of the life that I've been given exactly as it is, without wishing it was something else. I'm very happy. I enjoy my life absolutely. Qigong, through Master Wang, has given me for the first time a faith in something that I don't need to have explained, it just is.

I've had religious visions since I was a child. I started heavily studying meditation and Buddhism about 15 to 20 years ago. Ram Dass got through to me more than anyone because I don't have the sit-stillness to study in one laborious method. In Hawaii on my honeymoon, I stayed at the Maui Zen Center in the Roshi's bedroom while he was away. And I had a series of dreams that changed my life. And in the dream I was dying and trying to get to the light. And Roshi Aitken, a Buddhist master whom I'd never met, came running down the tunnel after me. He grabbed my hand and dragged me back out and he said, "It's just not your time. You need to listen to me. I know you don't want to and you're fighting it, but you have to listen and start paying attention to the practice." That was probably 15 years ago. He's very old and frail now. I learned about eight years ago that he's a writer, he's the Buddhist dream guy. People get around him and have dreams.

My experience with Master Wang has been very deep. The words that come to mind are love, beauty, peace, special, related. I am just going to continue to heal. Absolutely. When I have the fear—I know what fear is, and I always go with it—I let it run and watch it go all the way.

My brother almost died a couple of years ago. This is after I met Master Wang. And I knew that I was going to have to find the energy to get in the car and go to San Francisco and hold him and help cross him over, because otherwise he just wouldn't go where he wanted to go. I was getting ready to leave and I just threw myself on the floor and I thought, I haven't even met my own death yet! So I spent 45 minutes in deepest meditation and I allowed my mind to visualize every possible conception I could have of what it might mean to die of cancer, from groveling in agony to peacefully laying in wrinkled skin, a skeleton in a bed with a claw out, all of it. And the only place I could ever get to with any of it, any time, I would come right out of it and say, "I'm energy." That's the bottom line, I am energy. That's it, I AM.

So, fear is not I am. I do get scared to death, and I have to cope and deal with fear. But somewhere inside of me is this peaceful sense of beingness. I don't want to die. I love life. I am surrounded with living creatures. I thought about it yesterday, very deeply, about how much I want to live. I thought about all the little children laying in hospital beds with no hair, puffy from chemotherapy, and they want to live too. It's non-discriminatory. Life. Death. It just is.

A few weeks after our meeting, I receive a breathless call from Aiea. Her doctor has just received the results back from her latest tests and says there is now no evidence of cancer. An MRI shows that the mass in her abdomen and all of her nodes are gone, and that her ovaries and uterus are normal.

Aiea tells me of her latest dream. She was directed to go and find a red Qyan Yin. She's been looking but has not found one. She's decided to find an unpainted statue, buy red paint and paint it herself. Aiea has also decided not to return to school. She says it has become clear to her that she needs to spend her time meditating by her fish pond and writing children's stories.

7   A Puff of Smoke, Floating on the Wind

Children are playing along a tidy street of modest, older tract houses. The garage door is open and Mettie, a slight woman of 39, and her husband are inside the garage talking with a neighbor. Her husband is leaving to pick up a teenage daughter. Mettie invites me into the house through the garage door. It opens onto the family room. Stepping gingerly over sleeping bags I follow Mettie through the house. The dining table is filled with plastic trays of brightly colored beads, scissors, and other craft supplies left over from a slumber party of nine-year olds the night before.

Short brown hair frames Mettie's drawn face. Her voice is barely a whisper amidst the jumble of children bounding around the house. She evicts them from their video games in the living room and asks them to begin their Sunday morning cleanup as we begin our interview. She winces at the noise of boys vacuuming leaves on the lawn outside the window. Her home is a chaotic blur of noises. She warns me of her cognitive impairments, but I am impressed that she is able to carefully hold the threads of her story in spite of this scramble of energy.

There are photos on the coffee table of a smiling couple, of a young woman holding an infant, of her handsome husband proudly holding a toddler. Mettie now seems overwhelmed at her life and yet determined to once again pick up the pieces and reclaim her place in it. Mettie's face is earnest as she struggles to sort out her memories, to be coherent in her story. Her voice gains strength as she talks, although it rises and falls with emotion. Although her body language is that of victim, Mettie's eyes are direct and clear, and I see a great pool of courage within.

In November of 1997, November 26, I had my second major stroke. As it turns out I have a very rare cerebral vascular disease which is how, why we found out. I had two strokes, with this one. With this stroke I lost the vision in my left eye and the hearing in my left ear and also I lost the use of my left arm and my left hand entirely. When I was in the hospital I couldn't even lift my left arm up. And I lost some of the use of my left leg and foot. But not as bad as with the first stroke. With the first stroke I lost the use of my whole right side entirely.

The first stoke was four years before, that would be 1993, in December of 1993. Short term memory is my weak point. But this is long term memory. I can do that. I have had a lot of cognitive difficulties also. Memories precisely, short term memories. And also my ability to organize my mind has been a real challenge for me. I am a very organized person, to the point of being compulsive and controlling. So I've been affected cognitively as well as physically.

The first stroke affected me physically, it took out my whole right side. I had to learn how to walk again, how to use my right hand and arm and every-thing. But cognitively, it was nothing compared to this one. I am pretty darned stubborn, in addition to being willing to work hard. And I came back from that first one. It took me about four years to come back to the point now with my right hand that I could play some notes on the piano if I chose to do so. A friend eventually is going to give me some piano lessons. My left hand is also almost back to the point where I can do that. And that's going to be a new skill for me to learn to build more synapses in my brain. Which is what I am always trying to do, to rebuild the skills in my brain.

I started to see Master Wang after the second stroke. The first time I saw him was in Sonoma. It was quite awhile ago. Some friends said you've got to see this man. I saw him for the healing and also took a workshop, the Five Element Stake workshop. I actually wasn't aware that I had lost the hearing in my left ear entirely. Although my neurologist knew this. I asked my doctor, did you know that I had lost my hearing in my left ear? And he said yes. He must have told me of course. And after I saw Master Wang I told him that I could hear again, and he said that's great. He didn't feel the need to test for that. But he has been testing my peripheral vision and noticing that it has been coming back.

That very first healing I went to in Sonoma with Master Wang was when I realized I couldn't hear in my left ear at all. But the hearing came back just like that. I mean it really came back. By the time the healing was over, I was hearing people on my left side making little noises as people make, just the tiny noises that people make. I hadn't really been aware that I wasn't hearing these things, but all of a sudden I could hear everything out of my left ear. I had my cell phone with me. I had to call my family and use my left ear to do the listening! It was so exciting. That was the first big thing that happened. But the residual effects on my left eye have also been coming back. I don't have all my peripheral vision still. But that has been coming back a little at a time when I go to the healings. I went to a small group healing once in San Francisco and I think I got back a lot more of the peripheral vision at that one.

"Moya Moya" is the name of this disease. It's a Japanese phrase that stands for "a puff of smoke floating on the wind." When you have an angiogram it's the image one gets. The veins end up looking like there's a puff of smoke floating around there. I have an excellent neurologist in Santa Rosa and he's written articles on the disease and he's worked a lot with people who have the disease. I had brain surgery after the second stroke, in December of 1998. He has done this surgery a number of times. I am very fortunate to have western medical doctors who know about the disease and can work with it.

I told my neurologist about the Qigong and asked him if he would recommend going to Master Wang. He said, "Are you kidding, I'm the one that recommended vitamin therapy for headaches!" And as soon as I can get some information to him...My friend is a disciple, she's the one who got me going to Master Wang. She has the information I'm going to give to my neurologist so he can at least tell people about Master Wang. It's not that he's going to recommend him, just that he could refer people if they want to go.

Before I met Master Wang I did have the opportunity to see an osteopath. Thank goodness my mother had some money that she had stashed away. She paid for a friend to come and help take care of me at home, at my house. And she paid for me to see an osteopath. That was very helpful, it helped me feel more clear headed. It gave me a little more feeling in my hand. I did Feldencrist, a great lady from Israel who learned from Feldencrist himself. It was very helpful. It was the only other thing that gave me any help at all. I have a friend who is an acupuncturist. She has done some treatments on me mostly for my headaches and to help me feel stronger, as I was feeling just generally pretty weak. So she did some acupuncture for that kind of thing.

But Qigong is really the first thing that helped in a big way. I did both the healings and classes about four or five times. I've been able to do a couple more healings than that. I learned the Five Element Stake, and One Finger Zen One and Two. And I was able to take the Six-Syllable Mantra. I also go to the weekly Qigong group practice in Sonoma whenever I can.

I find that my energy level is always really low these days, but if I can just at least get up and do the Three Palms, that gets me into a state of Qigong well enough to be in a relaxed mode where I'm not in as much pain as I typically have. My neurologist won't call it migraine pain because it's vascular headache due to Moya Moya, due to my disease. It's a chronic pain, but we can't treat it as if it's migraine because with migraine the blood vessels open up and you have to take something to help them constrict.

The nature of my disease is that the arteries in an area of the brain tend to constrict. They occlude. They shut down. Three of my four cerebral arteries shut down when I had this stroke. My doctor was surprised that I was even walking. And I walked right into his office and walked right out of the hospital after I'd been in there 13 days, I think 11 days in intensive care. Well, I have my children to live for. And that makes a big difference.

During a healing I often times feel the band around my head sensation that Master Wang talks about. It's gotten to be a common feeling for me to feel heavy sensations in my head. But it's not like the pains, I still call them migraine pains. I see lights frequently. I see golden light a lot. Golden and white light. I think that might be what I want to see. I try to picture myself in white and golden light as a rule because that's my work right now.

Right afterwards I feel like I can breathe deeply again. Not that I haven't been able to breathe deeply, I'm just taking much deeper, cleansing type breaths. I feel like a burden has been lifted off my shoulders so to speak. Everything is raised up off my head, neck and shoulders. I carry a lot of weight there. I do carry a lot of tension in my neck and shoulders naturally. I always have. I'm a chronic work-a-holic. But I'm getting better. By the time I get home I'm usually ready to sleep for days. I just feel like I need another nap. I feel like the healing was actually work in itself. Clearly my brain has been working to heal itself when Master Wang was doing his work.

I have come to understand that the brain burns a lot of calories when it's working, when it's doing the work that it needs to do. Especially in situations like mine where it's working to heal itself. I'm aware that Master Wang is doing a lot of the work. He's taken a lot of the work on himself. But clearly my brain is doing its own part of the healing and I need to sleep, sleep, sleep. It's a good work feeling. It's not an exhaustion, like I'm never going to get enough sleep which I do feel sometimes. But just feeling like let me take a nap today, and get to bed early and have some quiet time. And on those days I do get my naps in, which I don't always do on regular days. This feeling of healing lasts a good solid week, up to 10 days. I haven't exactly timed it, but my feeling is that it lasts longer now.

Money is always an issue for me. I am not able to work right now. My mother was able to pay for the healings and the workshops for quite awhile. My husband works and earns adequate money, but we have issues around that. I think he hasn't seen enough progress to make him feel like it's worth the money. Discussing money with us... Actually at some point he decided he didn't want to be with me anymore....

Mettie's voice trails off, breaks, and she begins to cry. We are silent for a few moments as she reaches for tissue and struggles to regain her composure.

...We're working on that. At the last workshop I was able to go to I got a lot of healing around the relationship. I found ways that made it easier to be open-hearted towards my husband. Which is how I think I have to be in my life, approach things in a more open-hearted way.

I find that being able to get into that state of Qigong at all makes a difference. Over the years I've done different types of meditation regularly. For many years, since I was 14 years old. Just pursuing things. I felt I needed to meditate to find out what was true and that kind of thing. I have a regular meditation prayer. A combination of stuff. I ask my questions and listen for answers and take the time to gather the energy that's out there for me. I'm aware that Master Wang is out there for me. He said he sends energy for me and I take it.

When I saw Master Wang for the first time, I was neither skeptical nor more open and welcome to it. I am one of the most cynical people you can meet. But I also try to approach life with an open mind. Being in the situation I was in, I figured what the hell, it can't hurt. As long as it doesn't hurt. I have always been willing to try anything as long as it doesn't hurt. Even the acupuncture. I was feeling, I don't do needles well at all. I was so worried about the needles, but they didn't hurt, they really didn't hurt. That's the only healing that I've accepted that I thought might hurt. But with the healings with Master Wang, I was told that all you have to do is sit there, just sit there and relax. Relaxing is not an easy thing for me to do at all. But I did it.

I've been focusing on getting the use of my left hand back. After seeing Master Wang I've gotten to where I can touch my fingers to my thumb. I couldn't do that before. I couldn't even move my thumb. It was frozen. I've gotten to where I can actually move my thumb by itself. The fine motor obviously isn't back yet. But it's getting there. I've even taken a trip to Europe to visit friends. All by myself. With my two heavy suitcases. I got to go to Poland and the Czech Republic and I did fairly well all in all. And I came back on my own too. I handled all the situations just fine, even the cognitive stuff. The hand wasn't a problem at all.

I need to start focusing more on improving the cognitive stuff. I can't drive yet because I can't organize my mind well enough to feel comfortable on the road. I won't even try until I know I can be safe. I'm a defensive driver and I don't want to be one of those people everyone else is looking out for.

Qigong has given me a spiritual life that I have been lacking. I have always been a very spiritual person, but not a religious person at all. I'm not a joiner. But oddly enough Qigong has spurred me on to pursue Christianity with a couple of friends of mine. Just to look into it to see what it's all about. I wasn't raised with any strict religion and didn't know anything about all of that. So I'm looking into a lot of different things as far as my spirituality goes.

My friend who referred me to Master Wang, we have a drumming circle, a women's circle. We do journey, shamanic journey, somewhat like meditation. We have our power animals, and we have our spirits that help and guide us, that help us do our meditations as we need to. Essentially, Qigong has given me more strength to pursue that. It's given me another way to funnel Qigong through shamanic journey. And I can funnel shamanic journey through my Qigong. I find that while I'm practicing Qigong I can sometimes journey at the same time.

I contemplated Buddhism, I contemplated becoming a disciple of Master Wang. But I've just got to kill those flies. I don't think I could keep that precept about not killing any living thing. It's hard not to kill insects when you drive a car. They're all over your windshield when you get where you're going. If I was ever going to join something...I always tell people I'm not a joiner...and even with this whole Christian thing I'm looking into, I'm not a joiner. I did seriously consider about becoming a disciple, but the whole thing about not killing anything became too much for me. I just realized...the lying thing was fine, I could live without lying.

I do talk to the Devas (celestial beings) of the flies before I kill them. My friend and I have learned how to do co-creative gardening. And we speak to the Devas of the various insects and we say, "What can we do here? I need this to happen, how can we make this happen together?" I do talk to the flies and say, "Get off that wall. I can't live with you here and you should find another place to be now. Is there something I can give you to help you feel more comfortable some place else?" And sure enough, I can get an answer that way. Sometimes. I've been speaking to the Devas of the snails for years. We used to have them marching up the driveway when it's raining. It's like they're marching up in droves. I used to have a daycare center and I wouldn't let my daycare kids kill the snails. Some of them stepped on them. Yuck. But ants! Ants are out!

No, there were some Buddhist precepts that I just could not keep, so I could not have been one of Master Wang's disciples. It was not that I did not want to join Master Wang, I would have loved to be a part of his organization. If I had any spare energy at all I would have joined the society, the ITQA. But as it is, it takes all my energy just to get myself out of bed in the morning.

I have felt very fulfilled about being able to be around Master Wang. He touched me once, not inappropriately, just on the hand. He reached out and touched my arm or something like that and I could just feel the energy pouring right out of him. Electric. I felt overwhelmed by that in a very good way. Just so thrilled to have him helping me. And I'm not a fan type person. I'm not a follower of anybody in particular. I've never really wanted to meet a famous person, desperately wanted to touch them, or get their signature or anything like that. It's not like that with Master Wang. I just felt so honored that he would touch me in a healing way. I felt he shared his energy with me in that instant and was making extra efforts to work with me in my particular situation at that point in time. And so I was very moved by being there in the same room with him and being that physically close to him. None of this fan stuff. Just being able to experience his spiritual energy.

I'm so glad Master Wang is a part of my life. He's in my circle. I couldn't say he's my friend, but I'd love to be friends with him. He's always accessible. When I can't go to sleep at night which isn't uncommon, I ask him for help getting to sleep. Just having access to that energy and having access to the energies of the people in that weekly practice group too. I think we all share an energy together. I feel very much like I belong with Master Wang and this group of people.

8 Lessons For Living

On a narrow road in a coastal valley north of San Francisco I make a sharp turn into a driveway almost hidden among vineyards of thick purple grapes, gold and red leaves. Behind a tall hedge there are two houses, a small guest house in front, and a slightly larger house set back under trees.

A trio of red-winged blackbirds at the edge of the lawn scrutinize me as I step from my car. I don't see a front door, so I walk around the side of the larger house to a vine covered patio in back and knock on a sliding glass door. A stocky, muscular man with a stubby beard and short cropped hair, invites me in. He prefers that I not use his real name in this book and suggests I call him "Rod," a nickname his father used. He apologizes for the flowers, ribbon and other materials strewn over a massive pine dining table in his kitchen. They are left from floral arrangements he made for a friend's wedding the day before. His kitchen window looks south, across a wide expanse of vineyards. His own small plot is adorned with flowers and well-tended fruit trees. Later, he gives me a tour and sends me home with a gift of Comice pears, blushed with ripening pink, so succulent that they melt in my mouth when I eat them.

Rod's home is simple, but filled with beauty. Unadorned cement floors cool a warm fall afternoon. In the living room an *unfinished pine fireplace surround is elaborately carved with cherubs. There are other finely carved pieces of furniture, an antique sofa and chairs, but what strikes me most is the color of the walls. They glow with a soothing, warm peach hue that pulls all the rustic elements of his home together into an organized and pleasing whole.*

Rod is articulate about his illness and about the many lessons he has learned from it. He is eager to share his insights in the hope he may help others. His ruddy complexion and robust demeanor are at odds with the scarecrow he describes as himself a short time ago. He searches through drawers to find a photograph from that time. Unsuccessful, he settles into a chair across from me and begins his story.

The illness is HIV. And the day that you get your diagnosis, it changes your life forever. Tremendously. Like one day is completely different and you step into a whole new life the next day. I've done a lot of work with HIV patients, with people living with HIV, and I think it's fairly consistent that people experience never having a moment that you're not aware of it. Especially in the beginning when the media led you to believe that it was a death sentence. And indeed, everyone you knew that had contracted it was dying and you feel like your death is imminent. You tend to feel you're going to die in the next month. It's really overwhelming on so many levels. Both spiritually and in every day life.

I was diagnosed in 1990. It was an incredible blow in that many things happened that particular year for me. My father died. I had a pet dog that I was very close to and she died within a week. Everything happened within a month. My diagnosis, my father's dying, the dog dying. It was incredibly stressful. And I immediately broke out into herpes zoster, which is exacerbated by stress. It is a latent virus that is activated by stress. So all of that happened at once. Then, at the same time, I resigned from my business. I had built a national business. It was very successful. I had a partner and I left the business on a handshake. I was later betrayed by my partner so I never received anything from my interest in the business. And that ended up becoming a long, legal struggle. So, it was a very tough time. It was very difficult.

That was very early on. That was when they were prescribing AZT. I was inclined towards holistic medicine always and I resisted taking AZT. I tried all kinds of alternative modalities, including diet. Mostly diet, but I can't even remember. I sort of tried the therapy d'jour for a long time. I explored all kinds of things, and that in itself was overwhelming. Because everyone you talked to had the best of intentions, but they all had a different modality and all had different recommendations. I was equally torn to pieces by all of those choices.

It was very difficult to center on any particular method that you could have real confidence in because nothing had been proven to be effective and you were always thinking that you might be missing the boat or missing out on something else. Because everything involved a fast, or a certain discipline or a certain type of treatment. From energy work to herbal, just everything had it's own parameters. I did acupuncture, immune enhancement diets, cleansing diets.

At that point I just had an HIV positive diagnosis. For a long time I maintained relatively good health but with definite dips in energy, lots of energy fluctuations. Maybe six years later after the original diagnosis, my T-cells finally dropped to below 200 which classified me as officially having AIDS. So, with an AIDS diagnosis I was able to go onto disability. That helped to relieve some stress because it was very tough at that point to make it financially. Because as I said, I'd lost all of my financial resources with the business I'd built. And I had opted off of the group health plan because at that time, with small group health plans, insurance companies were raising the premiums for the entire group. They can't single out individuals, but they can raise the whole group rate. And I had some experience with friends who had small businesses that had just been priced out of affordability. So to keep my employees' insurance intact I had opted not to go on the plan. I was left without insurance or anything. So getting the disability status finally gave me insurance options with Medi-Cal, and that in some ways was a blessing.

My health would sort of reach plateaus, but I contracted a few opportunistic illnesses and those substantially diminished my health. At the lowest point, severe gastrointestinal disease had set in and I began wasting. I lost about 100 pounds. I became incredibly weak. I contracted pneumonia. The photograph I was looking for, I showed Master Wang once. It's a very dramatic photograph of how I looked at that point. Extremely dramatic, I was 100 pounds less than I am now. I was fed intravenously because I was too weak to feed myself. I remember, I was so weak that I couldn't lift my head to take a sip of water. I couldn't even turn my head. I was at home, I had in-home care.

Frankly, I thought I was dying. Everyone thought I was dying. So I remained in that state for a few months. I was also taking care of my mother. I was the only surviving family that my mother had. She's a brittle diabetic. She had a really serious episode in 1995 or 1996, and I brought her to California to live with me. So, I was also taking care of her at that point in my life. When I reached the point where I was really on the threshold of death, I consciously knew that I could just sort of quietly stop breathing and die. There was a day, there was a moment, that I was aware that I could have passed. But because of my mother and her care I did not want to die before she did. I was determined that I would somehow muster the strength to recover.

That was the turning point. I did somehow start getting stronger after that. I forced myself...from somewhere I found the strength to be able to start drinking again. Because I was dehydrating. My body was shutting down. It's actually a very peaceful state of mind. You're in a rather altered state at that point. That was a real interesting lesson to bring back from the threshold of death. There really isn't any fear or pain. It's actually very comfortable.

At that point, living was a very conscious act of will. Mostly because I felt like my time wasn't meant to be over. There were people I loved that I wanted to be here for. Like I said, my mother, I didn't want to pass before my mother. She would have had no one to care for her. Not that I was doing a lot to take care of her. I had a lot of other support at that point, friends helping, and my partner helped a lot. I am very indebted to him for all his help.

This was about two years ago, before I met Master Wang. I became very ill in the summer, around the end of July. So August, September and October were the months I was really suffering. By November I was beginning to recover. At that time I developed what I thought was a sore throat and started going in to see my doctor. He treated it for a number of things and couldn't find anything. Eventually he determined that it was lymphoma. So now, just as I was recovering, I suddenly had cancer of the lymph glands.

I met with an oncologist who is amazing. She was just out of Stanford and was very tuned in to the latest treatments. She decided that I would be a candidate for a very light course of chemotherapy on the presumption that people with HIV or suppressed immune might contract cancer more easily than a healthy individual and therefore might respond to a lighter course of treatment. They are aware that a heavy treatment can just do in a very ill person.

So I did chemotherapy that winter and I was just finishing up in January. I was reamed out from that experience. I felt hollow and just out of my body. It was a very difficult experience, as anyone who has had chemotherapy can attest to, but in my weakened condition I may have suffered even more. That's when I met Master Wang, right after that period. My energy was very, very low. At the first healing Master Wang turned my energy around. And after several healings, on subsequent tests there was no trace of the lymphoma.

The Santa Rosa Reiki Center was providing Reiki treatments for people with AIDS, and I was the only person that signed up. I was receiving treatments twice a week and one of the Reiki practitioners told me about Master Wang. I was initiated as a Tibetan Buddhist in the Kagyu lineage years ago by Lama Ole Nydahl, Protector of the Karmapa. He is a lineage holder who foresees where the Dali Lama is going to reincarnate. His teacher is the lineage holder known as the Karmapa. So I have exposure to Tibetan Buddhism and I felt very drawn to Master Wang because of that.

I was also initiated as a Sufi years ago. So I have always considered myself a mystic, involved with more esoteric teachings. When I heard about Master Wang I had an immediate hit to do this work, to go for the healing. It felt right. Through all that I had gone through looking and searching for treatments I learned that I pretty much had to rely on intuition and go for things that just felt right because the choices were unlimited.

So I went to a healing Master Wang was giving in Sebastopol. I was planning to take the afternoon workshop, but I was so weak that day that I received the healing lying on the floor. I remember feeling immediately energized and I felt a new freshness. When the healing ended and they broke for the lunch period, I walked downtown and had a Chinese meal. I went back in the afternoon to the workshop and it happened to be One Finger Zen Part Two, with the movements of fingers and toes. Master Wang taught it. He mentioned that this practice could be done by people who were very ill and that you could even do it lying down.

I had been suffering from a quite extreme case of neuropathy. Neuropathy is where your lower extremities—I guess it can happen in other extremities, but especially in your feet—have a sensation of numbness. The feet feel prickly as though they are asleep and circulation has been cut off, and they can be incredibly cold. It was during a time of the year when it was still quite cold, especially at night. Quite often, I was not able to sleep. I would get up and put my feet in hot water and I could feel the heat of the water with my fingers, but when I immersed my feet I had absolutely no sensation of the heat. Soaking them in this hot water my feet still felt numb and ice cold to the point where I just couldn't sleep. I tried sleeping with electric pads wrapped around my feet, but nothing helped.

Neuropathy tends to be more intense in the evening. So that night, after I had seen Master Wang, I was getting ready for bed. Usually, by evening my feet would get very uncomfortable. Suddenly I noticed, and this was dramatic, my feet felt completely normal! Only the slightest shadow, a faint tingling, but certainly no discomfort. The neuropathy went away completely that evening. The neuropathy is caused by medications, and of course I had to continue taking them, so eventually it did come back. But it never came back to the severity that I experienced it before. It's very slight now, not really noticeable. So I would say that my neuropathy cleared up after that first healing.

The other thing that happened after that first healing was that I immediately noticed heightened energy to the point where I could stay up all evening and feel completely energized. I knew something very dramatic had happened. Just from that one healing. Although I remember in the afternoon workshop Master Wang came around and did a correction of my posture and he touched me. So I imagine there could have been a transference of energy from that as well.

I started going to as many healings as I could. I've taken all the teachings at this point and have repeated most of them. And I go and practice with the Qigong practice group every week. It's my intention to do a daily Qigong practice, although I don't always do that. I had decided to ask for discipleship earlier this year. I was making preparations to do that and then my mother died. The funeral and everything was happening in the summer during the eleventh group initiation. I had prepared a letter, but circumstances just didn't permit me to follow through with everything. I just felt like I needed to opt out at this time.

I went to a private healing last spring. The sense I had in talking to Master Wang was that he could only pass as much energy as my body was able to take, therefore healing would be a process. After that first healing almost two years ago, I didn't notice changes as dramatic at later healings. I suspect that was because I had such a long way to go. I did start gaining weight. I gained all my weight back after that first healing. I still continue to do Reiki and I try to live a healthy lifestyle. All the other different modalities that I participate in would probably all like to take credit for my recovery, but I personally feel that it was the healing I received from Master Wang that had the most dramatic impact on my health.

My doctor, my primary physician, is a world leader in HIV disease. He speaks at international conferences and teaches. He is very western based but he is supportive of my alternative work. His stance is that alternative healing is not his expertise, it's not his training, so he doesn't get involved with that. But I have an excellent rapport with him and he is supportive. Also, to backtrack, after my recovery, about that time protease inhibitors were developed, and I did start taking a drug protocol for the first time. So of course western doctors would look at my recovery and say it's the protease inhibitors. And indeed it could be the combination. In Sufism, the healing order teaches that all things work, and I believe that all things do work, in varying degrees perhaps. I think all things contribute to healing.

The first few healings that I attended, I often fell asleep and I often slept through the healings. I would always hear the words, "you can open your eyes now," and I can remember just subconsciously tuning into the facilitator's voice to open my eyes. That was my experience in the beginning, but now I don't usually sleep, I just go into a very peaceful state of mind and that is typically what I experience. The most interesting thing that I experience now after a healing that I wasn't aware of in the beginning—and this began to happen after the small group healing—about three or four in the morning I would wake up and I would feel like I was getting a transmission from Master Wang. It felt like I was picking up something from his personal meditation either in the form of a teaching, or clarity on something. I felt very strongly that it was coming from him. I mentioned this to a disciple who works closely with him and I asked if he meditated at that hour of the morning. She confirmed that he did indeed.

Master Wang told me himself the last time I saw him that he intends to continue to help me. Recently he's sort of been overburdened with a lot of things but he told me that I was still on his mind and was included in his meditations. So I think when I feel those things they are indications. It's very inspiring and it gives one a lot of hope.

As a Sufi I am attuned to centering in my heart. When I met Master Wang and heard of his vision, I was incredibly moved by his intentions. The desire to give something to the west to balance the direction that western medicine is going in...I was very moved by his teacher's mission to do that. I was moved by Master Wang's compassion to want to share that type of teaching and knowledge, to build a Qigong center. And I was maybe most especially moved with his wanting to build a home for the elderly. Having taken care of my mother I was deeply affected about how sad it is, how lonely and isolated the elderly are in this culture. And it speaks to me. Master Wang's intention to do something about this just grabbed me like a rocket. I felt this was someone I would really like to work with. So that's what attracted me. It's one thing to have all of the "rocket science" of high level teachings that the Tibetans have, and then to see it in the world with the compassion and the heart quality. That really does it for me.

I don't practice meditation a lot. I think I've had many lifetimes where I've meditated and I think I'm kind of riding out some carry over from previous life practice. Comparatively speaking, I feel I live more of a meditative life than most people here in the west, but I don't sit and do meditation practice. When I first was initiated in the Sufi order, I had friends who were Sufis and I actually sang in a Sufi choir. The director was a Sufi teacher and he ended up giving me an initiation. All my other Sufi friends had been given practices. Their teachers gave them mantras and stuff to do and I always felt left out because my teacher never gave me practices or anything. I felt like the black sheep. One day we were driving back from Mendocino, my teacher and me, and he told me that my life would be my practice. And I thought that was an amazing teaching.

I'm not in the flow of a lot of money right now, so affordability has been an issue for me. I've been fortunate to borrow or have money given me when I needed it to do the Qigong teachings. It's my hope that the teachings will someday become available to anyone that wants them or needs them. Probably in the future things will happen to help in that regard. I'm sure after enough time people will probably bequeath wills and estates to this cause. But that's been a struggle for me now because I'm in the midst of my illness and I really want to participate. I want to have access to the teachings and I want to be able to practice. I'd love to be able to teach other people at some point. That would be wonderful.

I just have this feeling about Qigong, that it's helped. Its really hard to say because it's hard to define. It's hard to track it. My direction seems to be positive. I've experienced feeling stronger, more energetic. And especially on an awareness level, like receiving the teachings, the awareness just seems to be sharp and clean. I don't know if it's just my own spiritual progress. I just know that it all has a cumulative effect.

Something occurred to me when I went to the private healing last spring. I know that Master Wang's ITQA organization wants to raise money because there are these goals to accomplish like building a place to study and a center for the elderly. I thought well I would offer myself up as an AIDS patient to be healed and if there is a total healing money would never be an issue because it would gain so much attention that it would solve all financial problems. But it's my under-standing that there is a certain amount of karma, or destiny, involved so it may not be the automatic solution that it seems like it could be. There's so much attention on AIDS because it's seen as an untreatable illness. It just occurred to me that if anything could do it Qigong could do it. That seems feasible, but whether I'm the candidate for that to happen to, I don't know.

I would say the most profound aspect is learning what the east has to offer toward healing. For westerners energy work is not particularly well known or understood. It seems to me the west has a lot to gain from understanding this type of work. I feel that we are extremely fortunate to have Master Wang here to teach us. Especially considering there are so many forms of Qigong, and Master Wang seems to have a very high level form of this information. It's a rare opportunity. It's exciting for me to participate in this because I feel this form of Qigong holds incredible potential in relieving a lot of suffering. I also feel that it's absolutely necessary to create balance at this point in time. I strongly align with the need to integrate what the east can offer toward healing. It's really a very exciting time to be alive. I am really very happy to be alive.

It seems to me the question is whether people can have an open mind. It's just so frustrating to encounter a closed mind. My initial exposure to Tibetan Buddhism taught me that every moment is alive, exciting and full of magic and wonder. Just because it is. I try to remember that at all times. Actually that is what has carried me a long way through this illness. An understanding that there is all potential in every moment. And to always remember that. I have to give credit to Sufism and Kagyu Buddhism and now to Master Wang for the whole amalgamation of my own spiritual path. And for understanding that everyone's path is indeed an individual one. Following one's intuition and having an open mind is definitely the best vehicle I know to get where one needs to go.

A little over a month after my visit, I receive an early morning phone call from Rod. He is calling to share the results of his latest examination. His T-cell count has gone up to the highest level in four or five years, and his doctor can find no detectable traces of the AIDS virus. His doctor is amazed, but cautious. The word "cure" is not used in terms of this disease. But Rod definitely seems to have found a balance between eastern and western modalities. He is confident that this balance will allow him to continue healing and learning more lessons for his life's practice.

9 A Living Lineage

I awake early to prepare for my meeting with Master Wang. The meeting, scheduled for 10 a.m. at his home, has been set to provide me with information that he feels I should have in order to finish work on the final chapter of this book. Normally it's about an hour's drive, but this January morning it is raining heavily and I decide to leave at 8:15. Just as I walk out the door my husband, who has left for work a few minutes earlier, comes back to tell me that the radio reports an accident on the highway over the mountains. A big truck has jackknifed in the northbound lanes, the direction I am traveling, and the highway is closed in both directions just past the summit. This means that even if I were to take the old road up to the summit, it still might not be possible to get through. After a few moment's deliberation, I decide not to take my chances on the northbound traffic snarl, but drive south, then east, and then north, about a 50 mile detour.

In spite of the rain, the detour, my anxiety about being late, I park my car in front of Master

Wang's at 10:01 a.m. Due to a mix-up in scheduling, however, the translator never arrives. Without a translator it's not possible for Master Wang to give me his input, or for me to ask the complex questions and get the in-depth answers I was hoping for. But the meeting is not unproductive. We talk instead about how he wants me to proceed, the process of publication, discuss ideas for how the book should look, agree on the basic areas that I need information about. It is decided that we should both meditate on this chapter and then if needed schedule another meeting with a translator present.

Actually, I have been meditating for two months about how to organize and write this final chapter, but so far no words have come. In the week before our meeting I struggled even to come up with a list of questions to ask. My struggle brought back a memory of my very first brief introduction to meditation in a class I attended in 1979. We were told to visualize a wise person on a mountaintop, and then to visualize asking that person for one piece of wisdom that we could bring back to our every day life. I easily visualized the sage, who still comes to me in the form I call "Third Master," but every cell in my body was shaken to realize that there were no questions, there were no answers!

When I return from Master Wang's I sit down and begin writing. In my meditation that evening I return to this realization with a deeper understanding. Since there are no questions, no answers, I must listen attentively with my heart.

There is much that we as a culture have not learned about the relationship between energy and the human body, therefore we are wary of accepting the concept that energy can influence healing. In our western culture knowledge is most often respected if it is based on layers of information that have been independently compiled and validated by rigorous methods of scientific or academic research. We tend to doubt the efficacy of traditional knowledge, especially if it comes to us from cultural traditions that we do not well understand.

For many of us, the complexity of our modern world seems to call for an equally complex system of knowledge in order to maintain our health and the ability to function in our daily life. This can make it difficult for us to place our trust in the healing potential of a seemingly simple practice like Tibetan Buddhist Qigong. Although this method of self-healing seems new and different to us, it's important to remember that the practice goes back many genera-tions, passed down in an unbroken line from teacher to student since the time of Padmasambhava himself. One does not need to accept or adopt Buddhist philosophy to benefit from this practice, but it is helpful to understand a few Buddhist concepts.

My dictionary defines "Tantric" as the realization of the oneness of oneself with the visible world. It is my understanding that the word "Tantra" means continuation, and refers to a realization of the continuous nature of the energy of the primordial state. Tibetan Buddhist Qigong is based on the Tantric teachings of Dzogchen that have to do with the knowledge and application of this continuous primordial energy. In the west some new age individuals who may not be adhering to true Buddhist tradition have infused the word "Tantric" with sexual overtones. This may refer to the male and female energy specific to only one aspect of Tantra, and should not be confused with the vast energy that the Dzochen teachings refer to. Dzogchen teachings are passed on as oral transmissions or transmissions from heart to heart. In order to receive the teachings an individual must have the capacity to perceive the subtle dimensions of light and the precise correlation between the human body and the universe.

If we understand that an individual's internal energy is vitally linked to the external energy of the universe, then we can begin to see how they influence each other. For example, if our internal energy is compromised for any reason, it's like opening a door through which illness or disease can enter. As a realized being, Master Wang has learned through his years of dedication and practice to control individual energy, and he can influence external energy to the point where he can manifest "miracles" of healing—i.e., exert powerful influence over external disturbances or phenomena.

If we can acknowledge that all dimensions, whether material or subtle, are manifestations of our own internal energy, then it's possible to understand that each of us possesses unlimited potential for self-healing and self-development. Master Wang emphasizes that whether it's concrete and tangible or something really fine and intangible, we all have this inner strength or energy. As unrealized beings, we are limited by the material form of our body, but the energy that a realized being is able to tap into and move around in is not limited by time and space.

In Tantric teachings mantra, or sound, is considered the first of three stages of the manifes-

tation of the body's energy. At this stage energy itself is
intangible and invisible. The perceivable aspect is the
vibration of sound, or mantra, which arises spontaneously and brings in universal energy. By repeatedly
reciting the powerful syllables of mantra it's possible to
develop and learn to control and use special abilities. If
directed toward the human body mantra can be used
to clear the meridians, balance yin yang energy, and
improve health. Master Wang relates that through the
use of mantra it's possible to even help save people
who are near death, and bring them back so they're
able to get back on the path toward good health.

Light is the second, visible aspect of energy, but
this phase is still without form. Many photographs of
Master Wang capture the aura of light-filled energy that
often surrounds his body during a healing session or
during meditation. A being who has achieved manifes-
tation as a body of light can communicate and actively
help other beings. The "body of light" or "rainbow body"
that was discussed in Chapter One is an extension of
this capability and represents the ultimate realization
of the highest practitioners of Dzogchen.

At the third stage, the rays manifest the various
colors and shapes that we perceive as tangible form. If
these rays are recognized as projections of our own
energy, then we can be considered to have the pure
vision of a realized being. One who has through
dedication and practice achieved realization of all of
these stages, attains the potential to influence how the
body's energy manifests externally.

In conducting the interviews for this book, I was
struck by the fact that each person recognized as a

factor in their healing that Master Wang had shifted their energy on a fundamental level. Although difficult to quantify, each felt they had experienced profound internal change as a result of their sessions with him. Although Master Wang's powerful mastery of Tibetan Buddhist Qigong can initiate healing and even reverse the course of serious disease, continued positive result ultimately lies within each individual's capacity for self awareness. Master Wang also stresses that high moral character is of supreme importance in Qigong healing. My understanding of this teaching is that it is only when we can embrace and nurture the highest and most positive aspect of ourselves that permanent healing becomes possible.

In our modern world with its fast pace and focus on instant communication and immediate gratification, it's difficult for us to grasp a system of knowledge that offers us such immense potential. We rush in and expect to learn in a few hours what it has taken masters of previous generations lifetimes of practice to apprehend. Master Wang often says, "let things happen naturally." I have come to understand that this means that we must learn to become quiet, open our inner eye and observe ourselves before we can receive the deepest level of benefit from these teachings.

The word "Dzogchen" is defined as total (chen) completeness (dzog). According to Dzogchen we each possess the potential for total completeness, total liberation, total wellness—however we want to define it—within ourselves. Realization is the simple key we can use to unlock this potential. But realization is not something we can get from simply reading a book or from ordinary Qigong teachers. In order to fully develop our ability to work with our own awareness, we must receive the teachings as transmissions from a true master of the lineage such as Master Wang.

Lineage is the heart of Buddhist practice and the reason it is still alive after thousands of years. Buddhist teachers, or masters, must reach a state of perfect awareness before they are given permission to teach. Students must practice until the master is certain that the teaching can be flawlessly taught. This passing down of exact knowledge or wisdom from generation to generation exemplifies the "three gems" of Buddhism, the Buddha, the Dharma and the Sangha.

The master represents the Buddha, or the enlightened source who teaches wisdom and lineage. The Dharma is the teaching itself, the guidelines for the practice. These two, the Buddha and the Dharma, create the Sangha, a group of people who offer support and connection to the lineage.   The Nyingma lineage is considered the freest or most open lineage of Tibetan Buddhism with an emphasis on practice and meditation. In the Nyingma tradition it is possible to achieve Buddhahood in one lifetime. These Tibetan Qigong teachings from the Nyingma lineage have come down in an unbroken chain, an unbroken lineage of energy, directly from Padmasambhava to Master Wang and his Tibetan Dharma brothers. Their present day disciples are the end of the line for this knowledge and therefore hold a grave responsibility to safeguard the teachings and yet share them with the world so the lineage does not end with this generation.

In workshops when Master Wang is giving us the various Qigong movements, students sometimes press him for clarification of the smallest details. He will oblige us up to a point. But then he smiles and tells us, "learn through experience, practice through intuition." I take this to mean that these teachings are not meant to be dissected in intellectual discourse. Instead, each person must strive to be present in the learning and commit to keep these teachings present in our daily lives. The lineage has remained alive through all these generations because this information is most successfully transmitted not from mind to mind, but from heart to heart.

Master Wang tells us that as many stars as are in the sky is how much information is contained in our bodies. He also tells us that it's important for each individual to unravel this information in our own body. It's only when we manage to quiet our minds and open our hearts that we can best decipher and use this essential information for healing ourselves....and for healing our external world.

• • •

Since lineage is an essential component of these sacred teachings it seems important to include the path they have taken from ancient times to this fortunate first generation of western students to receive them from Master Wang. Although Master Wang has carefully checked temple records with his Tibetan Dharma brothers, there is some ambiguity as to whether Grand Master Khenpo Munsel was the eighth or the ninth lineage holder of these teachings. This ambiguity arises because there are various interpretations as to whether Yeshe Tsogyel or Longchenpa should be considered the second lineage holder after receiving these teachings from Padmasambhava, who brought them to Tibet in the seventh century AD. Yeshe Tsogyel is listed here as the first generation lineage holder after Padmasambhava and Longchenpa as the second. In this manner of listing, Khenpo Munsel is the eighth generation lineage holder of these teachings.

It is very difficult to accurately translate Tibetan proper names into English. There are often multiple English versions of Tibetan names, and even Tibetan Buddhist scholars do not always agree on a single spelling. These names of the Nyingma lineage were translated from Tibetan into Chinese, and from Chinese into English. The English versions used here are those that most closely correspond to accepted English spellings.

PADMASAMBHAVA, 7th century AD
1. Yeshe Tsogyal, 8th or 9th century AD
2. Longchenpa, 1308-1363
3. Jikme Lingpa, 1730-1798
4. Jigmed Gyalbai Myugu, 1750-1825
5. Orgyen Jigmei Chokyi Bangpo, 1808-1887
6. Lungtog Tanpai Nyima, early/mid-19th Century
7. Akar Wangpo, mid-19th/early 20th century
8. Khenpo Munsel, 1916-1994

Appendix 1

The Practices

Tibetan Buddhist Qigong is considered one of the most powerful of the many Qigong systems in the world. Although you do not need to learn the practices in order to receive healing energy from Master Wang, healing can be increased by learning to access one's own energy. Practicing regularly will unblock stagnant energy in the acupuncture meridians, improve circulation, enhance the immune system and improve metabolism. Through these unique practices one can attain peace of mind and balance the emotions. Even healthy people can achieve great benefit by practicing Tibetan Qigong. Regular practice can promote longevity, improve spiritual awareness and clarity of mind, reduce stress, develop creativity and unlock potential.

In traditional Nyingma practice there are nine levels, three outer Tantras, three inner Tantras, and three secret

Tantras. It takes many decades to study them all and achieve the highest levels. But Master Wang's teacher, the Grand Master Khenpo Munsel Rinpoche, instructed him to come to the west, consider the situation and then determine what to teach. The Grand Master also directed him to achieve the best results in the shortest time. Master Wang has selected the practices described below to teach to his western students.

You do not need to be a Buddhist to receive the wonderful results of these teachings. However, in second and third level classes some Buddhist philosophy will be discussed. Master Wang's Tibetan Qigong classes may be taken in any order, and may also be repeated for optimum benefit.

LEVEL I TEACHINGS:

Five Element Stake
The five elements of traditional Chinese medicine are wood, fire, earth, metal and water. In this practice the five elements are addressed in a certain order and relate to a particular organ or function of the body. The movements of this form of Qigong accumulate and balance qi and strengthen the body at the cellular level so that healing can take place.

One Finger Zen, Part One
This practice consists of nine different movements, practiced in sequence. These movements gather energy so it can be absorbed and used to heal and strengthen the body. The posture of the body and specific movements are emphasized so that the body and mind can be open to receive the energy.

Bodhidharma taught this practice to the elite Shao-Lin monks more than 1,000 years ago. Although not specifically Tibetan, Master Wang has adopted One Finger Zen into his practice because of its long history of effectiveness and because he feels it is the best practice from the Zen tradition.

One Finger Zen, Part Two

In the traditional Tibetan medicine view, all organs in the body are connected to meridian lines through the fingers and toes. In this practice, inner strength and healing are promoted through specific positions of the fingers and toes. Three different forms—standing, sitting and lying down—are taught so that this practice can be used by even the most infirm.

Patting Qi Along Meridians and Self Massage of the Face

According to an ancient Chinese proverb, if you practice Qigong without doing the closing movements, you get the reward but you "throw it in the water," meaning that you get no lasting benefit from your effort. These movements, done at the close of each Qigong practice session, collect the energy generated through the practice and stores it in the body. They also balance the body's yin and yang energy which increases overall health.

LEVEL II TEACHINGS:

Six Syllable Mantra

Ancient cultures of India, Tibet and China have used incantations and sound to cure illness and promote healing for thousands of years. This advanced practice, when used in conjunction with the other practices taught by Master Wang, can be a very powerful element of healing. The mantra teaching is intricately linked with the philosophy of Buddhism, therefore includes a meditation and purification ritual. Students are taught to use the mantra energetically.

Expelling Negative Energies

Tibetan Buddhism teaches that there are many energies that cannot be seen, but nevertheless have a powerful impact on people. Some of these forces are negative in nature and can have harmful effects on one's well being. This practice helps overcome these negative influences and promotes the achievement of one's highest potential.

LEVEL III TEACHINGS:

Vajra Yoga

Vajra Yoga is one of the precious teachings given to Milarepa. It opens meridians and an energetic location in the body of profound importance to enable one to achieve one's highest potential. Vajra Yoga is a very high level, formerly secret teaching.

Three Syllable Mantra

Also called Vajra Recitation, this is the fundamental mantra recitation in Tibetan practice. It is the source and essence from all of the Tibetan Qigong scriptures. Merely reciting the syllables is not enough. Through empowerment by Master Wang, one may call in the infinite time and space energy. There are many lamas and rinpoches still waiting to receive this empowerment and teaching.

Appendix 2

Other Voices

During his lifetime practice of Qigong, Master Wang has assisted many thousands of people in their healing. In the years he has been in the U.S. he has assisted thousands more. Many of these people were willing to come forward to share their stories of healing, but only a few could be selected for in-depth interviews. Excerpts of written evaluations and other follow-up comments from some of Master Wang's U.S. energy sessions are included here.

During a healing energy session Master Wang chants sacred mantras to project healing energy directly into the acupuncture channels of everyone present in the room. This non-invasive procedure helps to remove negative energy in the meridians, improve circulation, enhance the immune system, and improve metabolism. Each person experiences the healing session according to individual needs for self-healing and spiritual development.

Master Wang is renowned in China for his ability to send healing energy to thousands of people over vast distances. In 1998, on two occasions when he was out of the country, Master Wang sent healing energy to students who gathered at separate locations in the San Francisco Bay area. I attended the January session in Santa Cruz, and I was amazed at the power of the energy sent to us from so far away! Four comments about the remote energy sessions are included. This first one is taken from my own personal evaluation written at the conclusion of the January event:

"I saw skeletons...many, many bones...As I walked through them I felt peaceful, like they were all <u>my</u> bones from many past lives...I was allowed to take a large golden disk down from a high shelf...I held it carefully, then drank from it three times...As I swallowed the last time, the bones dissolved into golden dust...At the end I was enveloped in a silver, radiant mist...I felt very, very pure, extremely powerful...very whole and happy."

...Virginia (January 1998, Master Wang sent energy from Tibet)

"A need to rock...lots of breathwork, deep inhales, long exhales...I did not know was capable of holding my breath that long!...At one point I felt electricity coming from my hands...Lots of light...not so much seen as a feeling that I <u>was</u> light."

.....Karen (January 1998, Master Wang sent energy from Tibet)

"Much activity in upper digestive tract, burping...pain in lungs, intense...a period of feeling very hot."

.....Vera (January 1998, Master Wang sent energy from Tibet)

"Overwhelmed by the strength of the energy in room...became more and more peaceful...saw dark blue color at first, then a gold ball, then a yellow ball with some red around it." .

....Martha, chronic fatigue (July 1998, Master Wang sent energy from China)

"The first evening after the healing I noticed that my vision was becoming blurry while reading with my glasses...without my glasses I could see with almost normal vision...The next morning my vision was still improved, but by the end of the day it had returned to normal (needing corrective lenses)..Since the healing my hips and lower body have loosened up and are moving much more smoothly...a smooth flowing of my whole being...there is a resonance of energy from my forehead to my heart...I can feel energy descending down the front of my body from above my forehead as if standing under a small waterfall".

....Ron

"I have experienced a remarkable rise in energy...The first few days after the healing it was almost too much...I feel changed on every level, spiritual, emotional, mental and physical...My heart feels opened wider and I am experiencing a profound peace and happiness, an expansive generosity and urge to kindness towards myself and others...I feel a greater sense of distance from and resolution with my husband's death, and all the painful events that surrounded it...During the healing I experienced what felt like many lifetimes being compressed into a moment, and I was saying good-bye to him across all those lifetimes...It was a very powerful experience, to travel across time...to feel the connection...to let it go, to turn toward the present and choose the life I am living now...I am deeply grateful to Master Wang for helping me take that painful, long resisted step into the present"

.....Ginny

"Since last time, my energy has been getting more steady"

.....Phyllis, chronic fatigue syndrome

"I felt shifts in spine and hips...my fingers automatically went to meridian points and massaged those areas...I feel more balanced and stable"

.....Catherine, arthritis, spine curvature

"A sense of vibration in all cells, resonating to one tonal sound, and a sense of being healed...a sense of balanced joy...I heard the words 'change your belief, change your own DNA'."

....Jane, lump in breast

"I felt a tight warmth adhere to my face, from just below my nose, up through my hairline and across to the center of my ears...I then felt the sensation of cool water being poured down my spinal column, slightly wider at shoulder blades...the coolness remained for 5 to 10 minutes"

....Carol, rheumatoid arthritis

"I smelled fragrance...tears flowed from my eyes...I felt anger"

.....Michelle, depression and headaches

"I felt powerful feelings of energy moving through my body...I also felt a great deal of release...sounds came of their own accord"

.....Stephen, leukemia

"I coughed excessively at beginning of session...by the middle of the session I was breathing clearly"

.....Pat, asthma, congestion and cough

"Tears...lots of tears started to flow down my face...my face was washed in tears...Feelings and emotions that have been submerged deep within came flowing out...I got in touch with how much fear I live in...I felt energy flowing along my spine and a tight band of energy around my head"

.....Lori, bladder problems

"Over four sessions I've felt a significant opening in neck, shoulder blades and back, especially on the right side of my body...Also, a tendency towards depression has lifted and qi is moving through the body more easily."

.....Haleh, liver disorder, anxiety/tension

"I felt a lot of heat in my body...pressure and tingling around my eyes and the top of my head...After treatment I felt peaceful and energized...less pain in my back"

.....Jack, back and shoulder pain, depression

"This session I felt lots of energy in my feet...I felt like moving, tapping and stretching them...then the energy moved up my calves, then up to my thighs...pleasant and energizing...I saw aquamarine, violet and purple...I feel very peaceful and happy"

.....Valerie, varicose veins, sore feet

"Peace...an energy flowing into my head...I felt like it was 'cleaning' me on the inside...all my organs seemed to vibrate as the energy entered my head...I had a tight band around my head...I felt joy and peace...I felt loved"

.....Anna, depression, sadness and pain

"Lots of heat...It felt like I was in another place, like a big open temple...I saw Tibetan monks in maroon robes...I felt many emotions...releases such as sadness and grief...more openness...then a clearing of lungs"

.....Chris, congestion and chronic bronchitis

"The energy in the room felt like silk...I saw indigo, red and gold colors...I had the sensation of energy spinning inside me...My face and crown area felt electrified...many gentle rocking and moving sensations...very peaceful and comfortable...My back pain at the beginning was very noticeable...afterwards the pain was much less severe even after sitting for several hours"

.....Sue, back problems

"Pain in left shoulder and neck...my arms jumped several times...Towards the end I felt electrical sensation at base of my skull. After the session there was no more pain anywhere in my body...the energy was flowing better"

.....**Joan**

"I felt the tension and pain my body dissolve into a beautiful color of blue violet, then an effervescent glow of white and gold...Felt pulsing at crown and saw concentric circles above my head...then a throbbing and swishing sound and a pulsing of energy moving through my body...At various moments I felt a block of energy and then it would dissolve...I smelled gardenia fragrance and felt an intense feeling of love...I felt my body elongate and strengthen...I felt harmonics of energy in my body"

.....**Jacqueline, breast cancer**

"Head and neck ached...nose itched...ears blocked...eyes leaked but I was not crying...I needed to rub my face and head...I felt dizzy...At times I felt light or energy coming toward me...I kept seeing bees"

.....**Elsa, hepatitis C, liver damage**

"I initially experienced a release of much sadness and fear and trembling...I gradually tuned into a place of anger and tiredness of being so consumed by fear...I saw and felt colors of blue and green pulsating around me and through me...Light and sound spiraled around and down my chakra system...I felt my lower chakras cleanse and align...My kidneys and bladder have been constantly infected...I felt much energy and relief circulating there"

.....**Debra, chronic kidney and bladder disease**

"Many lights of all colors...internal sensations of ants crawling under my skin—in forehead, neck, throat, arms, legs...Sensations of moving heat and cold...Many visions of energy flows, smells of evergreen forests, tastes of electricity...wave after wave of energy...Many tears flowed"

.....Cecil

"Felt sensations and a sense of movement in my face"

.....Sue, Bell's palsy/partial facial paralysis

"I felt very relaxed and free...I felt a lot of energy. Twice, a big ball of energy came and I held it in front of me. The first time, I brought it into to me; the second time I spread it out to the room and further to the city, and very quickly the world, the universe. I've been coming to classes for almost a year, and I'm getting better and better."

.....Sarah, multiple sclerosis

"Warmth, calming...then felt compelled to stretch and move my neck and spine. This opened, clearly relaxed areas no previous exercise or therapy had touched."

.....Grant, histoplasmosis/glaucoma

"Profound peace, tranquillity and relaxation...After session, shoulders and knees are pain free. Hands with much reduced pain. Sense of deep blessing."

.....Anne, arthritis

"I was very tired from the chemotherapy...I felt waves of energy coming from within my torso up to my head. I got warmer and warmer...I began to rock from side to side..I still feel very warm, very centered."

.....Natalie, cancer

"Buoyant, peaceful energy, very light...It felt like old emotional hurts that had lodged in my body were activated. I could feel the emotional and physical discomfort but also felt a cleansing of my tissues and organs...Disconnected parts of my body/mind reunited and integrated."

.....Mary, digestive problems

"Tremendous release throughout...my body started moving and stretching. Sounds were coming out of me like clearing pipes or places of stuck energy."

.....Joan

"I was able to move qi immediately... my wrists and hands freed up for movement. I moved almost the entire time until my body broke a sweat, as if I were running a long distance."

.....Beatrice, repetitive stress injury, neck, shoulders, elbows and hands

"Felt very peaceful and fell asleep. When I awoke I saw the sky open and I was surrounded by warm, bright light, like I was in a tunnel of light. I felt sharp pinches, once in my thigh and again on my arm...I saw monks in orange, all kneeling...I was presented with blue moccasins."

.....Esther

"First, deep calm...then a low groan building to a roar, and a deep crying release. At one point a dark orange spot appeared...Later, a small irregular cobalt blue shape appeared and slowly grew larger until it filled my entire field of vision. I found myself repeating over and over, 'I want to love more and be more open.' I smelled spices and roses."

.....Susan, lymphoma

"My neck did a lot of grinding noises...the left shoulder became very painful, then left elbows and wrist...then back to the neck and down left side again, like a circuit. I feel very tired, like I have exercised a lot, but a calm and peaceful feeling."

.....Michele, cervical disc damage

"I felt very nervous when I came in, but slowly started to relax...the chanting voice relaxed me...I could feel my organs, like my liver, my pancreas, responding to the sound. Had many beautiful visions...saw colors around my body...saw snow mountains of Tibet...I found it very healing, and strengthening."

.....Edith, high blood pressure/diabetes

"My neck felt like it was 'unwinding' the whole time, like the whiplash was healing. My diaphragm and my chest were heaving...I felt nauseous, then the nausea went away. Tears flowed freely. Very nice, healing energy!"

.....Dina, whiplash

"Warmth, tingling...saw flashes of white and turquoise light. Saw a flash of golden light and smelled the aroma of incense burning. After the session, when we opened our eyes, I didn't see any incense burning anywhere, and I didn't smell it any more."

.....Frank, back injury

"I had a very intense first experience...I felt the space around me filled with energy...my eyes and body seemed to course with the release of the energy. My bladder and kidneys felt light, I became lighter both in weight and in energy color."

.....D.G. kidney/bladder infections

I was hurting for awhile, really feeling worse...then my whole body felt much energy entering...down the center of my body. I really wanted to sing, but I mostly hummed, finding the frequency that seemed to resonate with my healing. Both my ears drained...felt very good...a very light feeling in the room and in me at the end of the session."

.....Karen, tightness in neck

"Within miles of the hotel my ears became hot, my hands clammy! I knew it was Master Wang's energy...That night I was exhausted but I couldn't sleep...I cried...it felt as if I traveled between worlds."

.....Shara, AIDS, cervical cancer

"Much heat in my body and feet, a tight band around head...pain that moved around my body...sensations of lightness then heaviness...lots of light and colors...tears and laughter. At the end, my body felt very whole, tingling, peaceful and well-balanced."

.....Barbara, inguinal hernia, leg weakness

"My legs went weak, like I had a bad scare or bad news...I felt pressure around my head and around the tops of my cheekbones and nose...I saw a white light, then blue lights. Later I was very tired but serene."

.....Eloise, chronic insomnia

"I felt great heat and a powerful energy throughout my body...When he passed out the mala beads, even though I did not get one I saw with my mind's eye a great blue/white light coming from the direction he was in, and this light seemed to protect me from dark chi."

.....John, allergies

"Incredible heat...I felt so heavy I had to lie down...I fell asleep and was awakened by a beautiful gold light...and by my name being called out."

.....Nicole

"Extreme heat...I had to remove my sweater...I saw strong purple colors...then blue...I saw a body in which there was a moving skeleton."

.....Guy

"Felt and saw a sharp pain go through the length of my left leg. It was black and about an inch wide, tapering to a point at each end."

.....Pearl, high blood pressure

"A very, very heavy feeling in my body...extremely intense, like lead or stone."

.....Alan, prostate cancer

"I got very hot...I saw gold, white and purple lights streaming down the center of my body...I also felt a strong pressure on my head and around my crown."

.....Jim, tonsil infection

"I felt pressure around my head and a visual awareness of the Buddha with many colors emanating from his form...I felt great heat as in a form of high purification, and a sense of 'peace that passeth all understanding'."

.....Hilary

"At one point my feet felt so heavy I wanted to move them, but when I tried, instead of movement I only saw a vivid green and blue color swirling around them."

.....Catherine, swelling of ankles

"I felt vibrations from below the floor that reminded me of an earthquake."

.....Helga

"Fire, heat, visions of flames...intense excitement in every cell...body became a vortex of light, expanding and joining something greater."

.....Pam

"Peaceful, saw colors of purple, gold and blue...felt as if there was a gentle hand warming my insides...at times it seemed that I was spiraling in a tunnel of energy."

.....Renee

"Saw lots of white lights in the shape of triangles and snowflakes."

.....Mary

"The beads were placed around my neck by Master Wang...I could feel a wind spiraling around my neck and head that started from the beads...a white funnel of light spiraled into my left eye...I saw many lights...I felt refreshed and new and very warm inside."

.....Tazz, asthma

Appendix 3

Photographs

Light is the visible aspect of energy. Many photographs of Master Wang capture the aura of light filled energy that often surrounds his body during a healing session or during meditation. The photographs in this section that depict an aura of light surround-ing Master Wang have been taken by ordinary people with ordinary cameras at different times and places in the world.

Rings of energy surround Master Wang during healing energy session at Tibetan Buddhist Representatives Conference, Buddha Mountain City, Guang Dong Province, PRC, 1993

Master Wang demonstrates Qigong movements for young Tibetan lamas, northern Tibet, circa 1980's.

In meditation before Chenrezig (Qyan Yin), Buddha of 1,000 eyes and 1,000 hands, Shang Yeh Temple, Tibet, 1999.

A blessing ceremony for young Tibetan lamas, northern Tibet, 2000.

A Dharma brother presents Master Wang with a relic of Grand Master Khenpo Munsel, Shang Yeh Temple, Tibet, 1999. About 200 miles from Lhasa, Shang Yeh was the first temple of the Nyingma lineage built by Padmasambhava in Tibet

In a gesture of respect Master Wang bows over butter lamps in Padmasambhava's meditation cave in the high mountains of Tibet, 1999.

Although the climate in northen Tibet is harsh, medicinal plants flourish in certain areas, 2000.

(left to right) ITQA Secretary Brenda Chinn, Attorney Charles Law and author, Virginia Newton, 2000.